THE

POWER

ZONE

THE

POWER

ZONE:

Living The Spirit-Directed Life

TONY SIMPSON

iUniverse, Inc.
New York   Bloomington

The Power Zone
Living the Spirit-Directed Life

iUniverse books may be ordered through booksellers or by contacting:

iUniverse
1663 Liberty Drive
Bloomington, IN 47403
www.iuniverse.com
1-800-Authors (1-800-288-4677)

ISBN: 978-1-4401-2922-3(sc)
ISBN: 978-1-4401-2924-7 (hc)
ISBN: 978-1-4401-2923-0 (e-book)

Printed in the United States of America

iUniverse rev. date: 7/15/2009

In loving memory of my wife, Sharon, without question the most wonderful woman I have ever known.
May the angels sing your song to you every time you want to hear it.

Contents

TEACHING DIAGRAMS BY CHAPTER

INTRODUCTION

One of the primary purposes of this book is to make you aware that you can live, work, and play under the identical power of the Spirit that sustained Christ during His earthly ministry. This identical power was given to us at the moment of salvation along with our eternal security. While we cannot lose our eternal security or the permanent indwelling of the Spirit, we can, we do, and we will lose the temporary empowerment of the Spirit. We lose the Spirit's empowerment every time we sin, and we sin every day. Once we say "yes" to sin, we are out of The Power Zone and back under the power that controlled us as unbelievers, our old sin nature.

The power of our sin nature can lead us into three progressively degenerate "zones" of carnality. The fact that these zones of spiritual-death all rhyme with each other isn't an attempt to be cute or clever. The rhyming zones are actually an answer to prayer. I have known for 30 years that that there are at least three zones of spiritual-death and that we become increasingly degenerate if we choose to move from one zone into the next. When I first started writing this book I prayed that God would enlighten me with a set of descriptive terms that would make it easy for a baby believer to learn and remember the six different zones this book deals with. Within two days, I had all the terms. The spiritual-death zones happen to rhyme with each other because of what the Bible says about each zone. When I discovered that the recovery zone, "the Phone Zone", would rhyme with the spiritual-death zones, it was just icing on the cake! The Holy Spirit is indeed a genius with a sense of humor!

This book will tell you what spirituality really is, what it isn't, and document everything with scripture. It will tell you where you go when you are out of fellowship with God and what can happen to you if you decide to remain under the control of your sin nature. This book will also give you a five-level spiritual growth model that will help you see where you are spiritually and where you need to grow.

There has been no attempt in this book to inform you which version or translation of the Bible I have used for my scripture references. There is a good reason for this. I am blessed with the luxury of having a pastor (R.B. Thieme, Jr.) who prepared messages by studying in the original languages of Greek and Hebrew. Pastors who can do that are extremely rare these days. The difference between the original languages and modern translations is absolutely astounding! Although I have four different Bibles in my library, I have found no single Bible as consistently reliable as my own detailed notes from 40 + years of being taught almost nightly from the original languages. For cross-references to ensure accuracy I have referred to Lewis Sperry Chafer's Systematic Theology, to notes in my Scofield Bible, and to my expository dictionary of New Testament words. While that is undoubtedly "the hard way" to write a Christian book, I am convinced it is the best way to insure accuracy.

You will discover that this book is full of teaching diagrams. Most if not all of the diagrams are accompanied by scripture references. I encourage you to take the time to look up and read the scripture references that accompany the diagrams as they will reinforce your learning experience. Bon voyage!

ACKNOWLEDGMENTS

As you begin to read this book, you will become aware of the many teaching diagrams. The first of these in chapter 1 is the diagram of the top and bottom circles, which I have named the Security Zone and the Power Zone. I first saw this diagram in somewhat different form in a Bible class in 1964 taught by Col. R. B. Thieme Jr. The colonel was pastor of Berachah Church in Houston for fifty-three years. The brainpower behind diagram 1 is Col. Thieme's, not mine. My late wife and I attended the colonel's Bible classes almost nightly from 1964 until 1994, when we moved to another city for a position change in my career as a coach and classroom teacher.

I modified and adapted many of the diagrams in this book from aspects of Thieme's ministry, to illustrate the subject matter of this book. Without Thieme's ministry, *The Power Zone* could never have been written. To say that I am grateful is a colossal understatement. I have remained under Thieme's ministry for the past forty-four years through audio recordings, and I will continue to use that ministry as a major inspiration although he is no longer teaching due to health concerns. Berachah Church is now in the very capable hands of the colonel's son, Robert B. Thieme III, who succeeded his father as pastor in 2004.

Because of the colonel's unprecedented, superhuman schedule of studying and teaching, I am the grace recipient of Bible training that money cannot buy and degrees cannot confer, as are countless pastors and churchgoers. The colonel's mastery of Greek and Hebrew gave him an insight into the scriptures that remains unmatched in the modern era. The very title of this book, *The Power Zone*, is a simplified term for what Col. Thieme named "The

Divine-Dynasphere" many years ago. For further information on his ministry, see www.rbthieme.org.

Over the years I have become aware that many Christians today are not familiar with Thieme's ministry. The primary reason for this is that his Bible study materials, although available, are not for sale. You can't find them at your local Christian bookstore. Still, Thieme's ministry spans the globe. His Bible study materials have been translated into at least ten different languages and probably represent the largest ministry emanating from a single church in modern history. Those blessed by this ministry probably number far into the millions. So if this book should happen to bless your life in any way, I can take very little credit for it.

Although I have not quoted directly from their works within the context of this book, in my studies I routinely use my eight-volume set of Lewis Sperry Chafer's *Systematic Theology* and my *Scofield Reference Bible* as double and triple checks to ensure accuracy of interpretation. Dr. Chafer and Dr. Scofield were close friends, and Col. Thieme frequently referred to them in his Bible classes. Col. Thieme studied under Dr. Chafer at Dallas Theological Seminary. Dr. Chafer founded DTS in 1924 and served as president from its beginning until his death in 1952.

I would also like to acknowledge and thank family and friends who have continuously encouraged me over the past year and a half not only to finish this book but to return to teaching Bible classes once it is done. Your encouragement and your prayers have meant more than you know. They have been a reminder of how important family and friends are when you are venturing into the uncharted territory of writing your first book.

CHAPTER 1: INTRODUCING THE POWER ZONE

The Historical Significance of Power and Integrity

POWER– What an interesting word! Many want it, yet few can handle it. Consider the extent to which angelic and human history have revolved around the concept of power. For example, Satan thought he would be like the Most High God, but because of his arrogant power lust, he was banned from heaven and thrown down to Earth. God deals with human arrogance in a similar manner. The first United Nations building, the Tower of Babel, was destroyed by the Trinity and the population of the earth scattered into separate nations because, like Satan, they wanted the power of God instead of a relationship with God. Under the Divine provision of "nationalism," God scattered the collective sin natures of man into separate nations for the express purpose of isolating evil.

Under the same satanic influence today, nations attack their own national sovereignty through internationalism. But God retains the protective provision of nationalism throughout the Church Age and even during the future Millennium when Satan is bound in the abyss and Christ personally reigns on the earth for 1000 years:

> *Rev. 20:1–3 – And I saw an angel coming down from heaven ... and he laid hold of Satan and bound him for a thousand years, and threw him into the abyss ... that he should not deceive the nations any longer until the thousand years were completed ...*

Christ was nailed to the cross as a result of the abuse of power by Jews and Romans, yet their abuse of power fell right into God's plan for salvation. Nations, governments, politicians, unbelievers, and believers—none are independent of the power and the plan of God.

> *Prov. 19:21 – Many are the plans in a man's heart, but it is the Lord's purpose that prevails.*

For abusing power, national economies have been ruined, governments destroyed, politicians disgraced, individuals imprisoned, and Christians severely disciplined by God.

> *Heb. 4:13 and Rom. 3:19 – And there is no creature hidden from His sight, but all things are naked and open to the eyes of Him to whom we must give account ... and all the world may become accountable to God.*

On the other hand, blessed by the use of power in accordance with God's word, nations have risen to great spheres of influence, governments have been sustained, statesmen respected, individuals prospered, Christians blessed, and millions upon millions blessed by association with them.

> *Prov. 8:15, 16, 18; Gal. 3:8 – By Me kings reign ... princes and nobles rule.... Riches and honor are with Me ... all the nations shall be blessed in you ...*

It is said that power corrupts and absolute power corrupts absolutely. There is no argument that the greater the power, the greater the opportunity for corruption. That is why America's Founding Fathers limited the power of government through the Constitution, the greatest governing document ever devised by the hands of man. But power can be a blessing or a curse, depending entirely upon the integrity of those wielding it, be it governing bodies or individuals. So the real issue is not power itself but the integrity of those entrusted with it. Personal power minus integrity is a force for evil. Personal power plus integrity is a force for good.

Uniting the New Believer with Perfect Power and Integrity

What is the source of the personal power and integrity for living the Christian life? At the moment of our salvation, the Holy Spirit placed us into permanent union with Jesus Christ, the perfect mixture of power and integrity. This permanent union occurs inside the top circle in Diagram 1. Simultaneously, we were placed into temporary relationship with the Father through the empowerment of the Spirit inside the bottom circle. Galatians 5:25 tells us that there are two different relationships: "living by the Spirit," in the top circle, and "walking by the Spirit," in the bottom circle. "Living by the Spirit" refers to our permanent relationship, and "walking by the Spirit" refers to our temporary relationship. Diagram 1 illustrates both relationships:

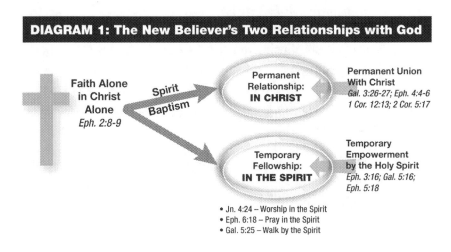

DIAGRAM 1: The New Believer's Two Relationships with God

Faith Alone in Christ Alone
Eph. 2:8-9

Spirit Baptism

Permanent Relationship: **IN CHRIST**

Permanent Union With Christ
Gal. 3:26-27; Eph. 4:4-6 1 Cor. 12:13; 2 Cor. 5:17

Temporary Fellowship: **IN THE SPIRIT**

Temporary Empowerment by the Holy Spirit
Eph. 3:16; Gal. 5:16; Eph. 5:18

• Jn. 4:24 – Worship in the Spirit
• Eph. 6:18 – Pray in the Spirit
• Gal. 5:25 – Walk by the Spirit

As any complete Bible concordance will reveal, the term *in Christ* can be found only in the New Testament, where it occurs over fifty times. The fact that we don't find this term anywhere in the Old Testament makes it clear that the relationship in the top circle is only for Church Age believers. (Church Age: the period of time between Pentecost and the Rapture of the Church) Likewise, the term *in the Spirit* is a brand-new relationship reserved only for Church Age believers. Old Testament believers were never commanded to be filled with or controlled by the Spirit in the bottom circle. That status was not available to them, because Christ had not yet been glorified by being seated at the right hand of the Father:

> *John 7:39 – ... the Spirit was not yet given, because Jesus was not yet glorified.*

However, New Testament believers are commanded at least twenty-five times to be under the control or the empowerment of the Holy Spirit. Therefore, as Church Age believers, we are absolutely unique in human history:

> *2 Cor. 5:17 – Therefore if any man is in Christ, he is a new creature; the old things [old relationships with God] passed away; behold new things [new relationships with God] have come.*

As Christ had prophesied during His earthly ministry (Jn. 14:20; Acts 1:5), the Baptism of the Spirit verified the arrival of the new Church Age (Acts 2:1–4 and 11:15–17). After Pentecost, the Baptism of the Holy Spirit for the Church Age believer is not "an experience," because it is neither seen nor felt. It is a one-time status-bringing event that can't be improved upon by any act of man. The Baptism of the Spirit puts us into permanent union with Christ in the top circle and therefore provides the opportunity to be empowered by the Spirit in the bottom circle.

God's Two Greatest Grace Provisions for Living the Christian Life

As we advance to diagram 2, we will see that salvation places us in two very different but inseparably related Divine design zones—a permanent Security Zone and a temporary Power Zone. The Security Zone guarantees an eternal relationship with God, while the Power Zone guarantees the power to live the Spirit-Directed Life. The Power Zone is the only place we can reproduce the character of Christ through the process of spiritual growth. Therefore, the Power Zone is God's greatest grace provision for living the Christian life.

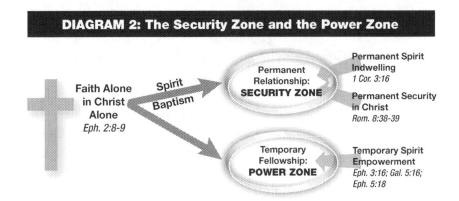

The Christian way of life is a supernatural way of life and therefore demands a supernatural means of execution. That supernatural means is the Power Zone ministry of the Holy Spirit.

The purpose of this book is to open your eyes to the power of the Holy Spirit that God has made available to every believer in Christ. The power of the Holy Spirit is exactly what sustained the humanity of Christ during His earthly ministry. This very same power was given to us at the moment of salvation, along with our eternal security. While we cannot lose our eternal security or the permanent indwelling of the Spirit in the top circle, we can, we do, and we will lose the temporary empowerment of the Spirit in the bottom circle. We lose the Spirit's empowerment every time we sin, and we sin every day. Once we say yes to sin, we are out of the Power Zone and back under the power that controlled us as unbelievers, our old sin nature.

Restoring Fellowship with God after Sin

God was well aware of our sin problem in eternity past and therefore made a grace provision for getting back into the Power Zone after sin. This grace provision has zero human merit attached, has nothing to do with emotion or guilt, and requires us to perform no acts of ritual or penance. We cannot make anything up to God, nor does God require us to. However, He does require us to utilize His grace provision for restoring fellowship with Him after we sin. How do we that?

We restore fellowship with God after sin simply by naming or confessing our sins directly to Him. Therefore, the grace privilege of naming our sins to God is the second greatest grace provision for living the Christian life. Why? For two reasons:

1. Since God is absolute righteousness, He can have nothing to do with sin. Sin defiles us before God, separating us from Him.

2. Confessing our sins to God is the only thing that frees Him to cleanse us and put us back inside the Power Zone under the Spirit's control.

> *Mark 7:21–23 – For from within, out of the heart of men, proceed the evil thoughts and fornications, thefts, murders, adulteries, deeds of coveting and wickedness, as well as deceit, sensuality, envy, slander, pride and foolishness. All of these evil things proceed from within and defile the man.*

> *1 Jn. 1:9 – If we confess our sins, He is faithful and righteous to forgive us our sins and to cleanse us from all unrighteousness.*

> *1 Cor. 11:31 – If we judge ourselves, we will not be judged.*

> *2 Cor. 7:1 – Therefore beloved, having these promises let us cleanse ourselves from all defilement of flesh and spirit, perfecting holiness in the fear of God.*

If we fail to name our sins to God, we remain out of fellowship with Him, out of the Power Zone, and under the power of our sin nature instead of the power of the Holy Spirit. Why is this so? Partly because sin defiles us before God, resulting in loss of fellowship, and partly because sin causes loss of empowerment due to grieving and quenching the Spirit. Diagram 3 should help explain.

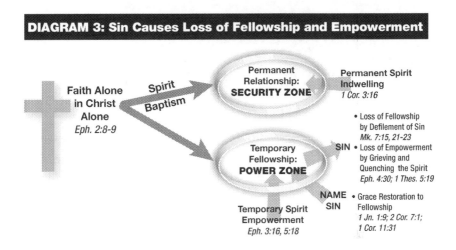

DIAGRAM 3: Sin Causes Loss of Fellowship and Empowerment

Once we are out of the Power Zone as the result of sin, we are in one of the three spiritual death zones powered by our sin nature. Regardless of which spiritual death zone we are in, it is impossible to recover the power of the Spirit without utilizing God's grace provision for doing so—naming our sins. This grace provision for restoring fellowship with God will be heavily documented in this book. You will not understand Diagram 4 now, but it will give you a panoramic view of what the study of the spiritual death zones will eventually cover.

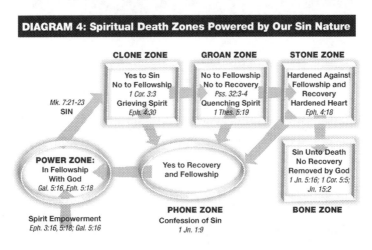

DIAGRAM 4: Spiritual Death Zones Powered by Our Sin Nature

Coining Some Phrases: The Spiritual Death Zones Plus the Phone Zone

I have named the spiritual death zones based on how they are described in the Bible.

1. **The Clone Zone.** When we say yes to sin, we grieve the Holy Spirit and therefore lose the Spirit's empowerment and our fellowship with God. At that moment, we enter the Clone Zone by placing ourselves back under the power of our old sin nature, the only empowerment we knew as an unbeliever. The Bible calls this "walking like mere men." Therefore, we have cloned ourselves under our old power source.

> *1 Cor. 3:3 – ... for you are still carnal. For where there is envy, strife and divisions among you, are you not carnal and walking like mere men?*

2. **The Groan Zone.** When we refuse to confess our sins and recover our fellowship with God in the Clone Zone, we quench the Spirit and enter the Groan Zone, further alienating ourselves from God. David recalls his time in the Groan Zone when he refused to confess his sins to God.

> *Pss. 32:3 – When I kept silent, my bones grew old through my groaning all the day long.*

3. **The Stone Zone.** When we still refuse to confess sins and recover our fellowship with God in the Groan Zone, we are hardening our hearts against Him. If this process of avoiding recovery continues, we will eventually enter the Stone Zone, even further alienating ourselves from God.

> *Rom. 2:5; Heb. 4:7 – But in accordance with your hardened and unrepentant heart, you are treasuring up for yourself wrath in the day of wrath and*

*revelation of the righteous judgment of God.... Do
not harden your hearts.*

4. **The Bone Zone.** When we refuse to recover from the Stone
Zone, God has the option of placing us under penalty of "the sin
unto death." If He does, we become bone minus flesh.

> *1 John. 5:16b; 1 Cor. 5:5 – ... there is a sin unto
> death. Deliver such a one to Satan for the destruction
> of the flesh.*

5. **The Phone Zone.** When we desire to recover fellowship
with God and return to empowerment by the Spirit inside the Power
Zone, God makes a very simple grace provision for doing so. To
return to the Power Zone, we simply use the "phone-home" prayer
by confessing our sins directly to God (1 John. 1:9). We will examine
why God graciously makes recovery of fellowship with Him so
simple in Chapter 4, "The Phone Zone."

Notice in diagram 4 that there is no recovery from the Bone Zone.
Believers in this zone are still saved and will still spend eternity in
heaven, but they have "blown it" in life, with the inevitable results
of loss of happiness, loss of life, loss of blessings in time and eternal
rewards.

Notice the way the arrows are pointed in diagram 4. If we are in
the Groan or Stone Zones, God does not require us to first go back
into the Clone Zone. We can go directly to the Phone Zone from
three of the spiritual death zones and get back into fellowship with
God immediately, back into the Power Zone. Is that grace or what?

Please be aware that living in the spiritual death zones is
accompanied by varying degrees of Divine discipline, depending
upon the severity and frequency of sin, plus the amount of time
logged out of fellowship with God (outside of the Power Zone). We
will cover this in detail in chapter 7. The issue of Divine discipline

is made very clear in Heb. 12:5–11, but verse 6 pretty well sums up the passage:

> *Heb. 12:6 – For whom the Lord loves He disciplines, and skins alive with a whip every believer who He receives.*

The believer is encouraged by analogy in Heb. 12:12–13 to go to the Phone Zone immediately after sin:

> *... lift up the hands that hang down ... make straight paths for your feet ...*

Notice from diagram 4 that the shortest path to recovery from sin is from the Clone Zone. While we can certainly recover fellowship with God from the Groan and Stone Zones, those respective paths back to the Phone Zone will likely be accompanied by a greater degree of Divine discipline, because we have been out of fellowship longer. If we remain out of the Power Zone long enough, we will obviously need a refresher course on basic doctrines related to living the spiritual life.

> *Heb. 5:12 – For though you should be teachers by now, you need someone to teach you the elementary principles of the doctrines of God, and you have come to need milk and not solid food.*

Therefore, the wise believer keeps very short accounts with God by naming sins immediately, every day. It is the believer who fails to name sins who falls into increasingly difficult circumstances that make spiritual recovery much more difficult.

The Real Issue after Salvation: Spirituality versus Carnality

If we are in any of the spiritual death zones, we are said to be carnal instead of spiritual:

1 Cor. 3:1 – And I could not speak to you as spiritual believers, but as to carnal believers, as to immature believers in Christ.

This brings up the central issue of this book, which is spirituality. Most churches today teach salvation correctly, that we are saved by grace and not by works. However, many churches have been deceived into believing that while salvation is by grace, spirituality is by some system of works. Not only is this absurd, spirituality by works is what the religious Jews tried to do through the Mosaic Law. It didn't work for them, and it certainly won't work for us. The absolute soul-state of spirituality is only obtainable through the grace provision of God. So, exactly what is spirituality?

> Spirituality is nothing more or less than being in the Power Zone through the grace provision of confession of sin.

Basically, spirituality is the absolute state of soul in which we are controlled by the Holy Spirit inside the Power Zone. Being in the Power Zone requires us to use the grace provision of naming our sins, which has nothing to do with works. Naming our sins is God's only grace provision for recovering fellowship with Him so that we can live the Spirit-Directed Life. Obviously, confession requires that we know what sin is. To most believers, sin is something that is done or said. However, the Bible makes it clear that all sin is first a thought, not necessarily something that is done or said. Remember that Prov. 23:7 says that as a man thinks in his heart, so he is. Therefore, at any given moment after salvation, we are either carnal or spiritual, based first of all upon what we think.

Important Questions

Failure to understand how to gain access to the Power Zone means that many Christians today are simply attending church and living out the warning of 2 Tim. 3:5 …

> *... having a form of Godliness, but denying the power thereof ...*

In other words, many believers are going through the motions of Christianity without utilizing the power of the Spirit because they are never in fellowship with God through confession of sin. Are you living your Christian life like that–powerless? Do you know how to access the Power Zone? Are you just going through the motions, just observing the rituals and substituting morality for spirituality? Do you lack the "spiritual dynamics" that accompany the Spirit-Directed Life?

> *Gal. 5:17 – For the flesh sets its desire against the Spirit, and the Spirit against the flesh, for these are in opposition to one another, so that you may not do the things that you please.*

Do you feel as though you need to be listening to God, but that God is not talking to you?

> *Psalms 130:1–2 – Out of the depths I have cried to you, O Lord. Lord, hear my voice! Let your ears be attentive to the voice of my supplications.*

Do you have a hard time keeping your "spiritual priorities" straight? Do you keep returning to your areas of weakness?

> *Heb. 12:1 – ... let us lay aside ... the sin that so easily enslaves us, and run with endurance the race that is set before us.*

Do you run out of "spiritual power" by the middle of the week?

> *Luke 21:26 – ... men fainting from fear and the expectation of the things coming ...*

Are you interested in greater meaning, purpose, and definition in your Christian walk?

> *Romans 12:2; Eph. 4:22–24 – And do not be conformed to this world, but be transformed by the renewing of your mind ... lay aside the old self which is being corrupted ... be renewed in the spirit of your mind ... and put on the new self ...*

If the answer to even one of these last few questions is yes, then you are reading the right book!

The Importance of Spiritual Growth

Is the Christian life really as simple as staying in the Power Zone? Yes and no. Getting back into the Power Zone is as simple as naming our sins. However, remaining in the Power Zone is the hard part because it requires spiritual growth. Numerous passages remind us that the primary objective of the Christian life is to reach spiritual maturity:

> *Eph. 3:16–19 – ... be strengthened in the inner man; so that Christ may dwell in your hears through faith; and that you, being rooted and grounded in love, may be able to comprehend with all the saints what is the breadth and length and height and depth, and to know the love of Christ which surpasses knowledge, that you may be filled up to all the fullness of God.*

> *Eph. 4:13, 15, 23 – ... until we all attain to the unity of the faith, and of the knowledge of the Son of God, to a mature man, to the measure of the stature which belongs to the fullness of Christ ... we are to grow up in all aspects unto Him ... that you may be renewed in the spirit of your mind.*

> *2 Pet. 3:18; Rom. 12:2 – But grow in the grace and knowledge of our Lord and Savior Jesus Christ ... be transformed by the renewing of your mind ...*
>
> *John 15:16; Col. 3:10; 2:7 – I chose you and appointed you that you might advance and bear fruit ... put on the new self ... being renewed to a true knowledge ... having been firmly rooted and built up in Him and established in your faith ...*
>
> *Col. 1:9–10 – ... that you may be filled with the knowledge of His will in all spiritual wisdom and understanding ... bearing fruit in every good work and increasing in the knowledge of God.*

Spiritual growth changes you from the inside out because it changes what you think, and that's what changes your words and deeds. Spiritual growth requires persistently subjecting yourself to accurate Bible teaching on almost a daily basis. Why daily? Because the rate of spiritual growth must exceed the rate of being corrupted by the devil's world, and the world is becoming increasingly corrupted by the devil. The rate of learning doctrine must exceed the rate of forgetting it. The amount of time spent inside the Power Zone must exceed the amount of time spent inside the spiritual death zones.

Chapter 1 is designed as a brief overview of the contents of this book. Some of the diagrams and verses in the first chapter will be repeated for clarification in other chapters because spiritual information is too important to be presented once and then forgotten.

This first chapter should make it clear to you that God has provided a way to empower and bless us right in the middle of the devil's world. However, God can only help us when we remain inside the Power Zone that Christ modeled for us. The Christian life is basically a choice of where we want to live, spiritually speaking. On a daily basis, we choose to live either inside the Power Zone or inside the spiritual death zones. We choose to either imitate Christ, Eph. 5:1, or the unbeliever, 1 Cor. 3:3. We are in constant spiritual warfare, and the battle is for our souls. The stakes of this battle are high: our inner happiness, blessings in time, and rewards in eternity. The only way we can win this battle is to live where God planted us, inside the Power Zone.

Because of the creative terminology used within this book, you would be wise to refer frequently to the glossary beginning on page 187. This book is designed both to introduce you to the Power Zone and to help you live, work, and play inside of it. May the Power Zone be with you!

CHAPTER 1 KEY POINTS

- The Christian life is supernatural and therefore demands a supernatural means of execution—God the Holy Spirit. (p. 5)
- We are commanded at least twenty-five times in the New Testament to be under the power of the Holy Spirit. (p. 4)
- The Security Zone guarantees an eternal relationship with God. (p. 4)
- We enter the Security Zone through faith alone in Christ alone. (Diagram 2, p. 5)
- The Power Zone guarantees the power to live the Spirit-Directed Life. (Diagram 2, p. 5)
- We leave the Power Zone by personal sin and re-enter it by confession of sin. (Diagram 3, p. 7)
- Failure to confess sin opens the door to all of the spiritual death zones. (Diagram 4, p. 7)
- "Spirituality" is being inside the Power Zone through the grace provision of confession of sin. (p. 11)

CHAPTER 2: INCREASING AWARENESS OF THE POWER ZONE

Our Greatest Grace Provision: The Power of the Spirit

In the business world, we are aware of those who seem to have "the magic touch"—everything they touch seems to turn to gold. It should bring a smile to our faces to see human genius or human talent at work in any profession. We have all known people who are set apart from the masses because of their ability to consistently make the right decisions and do the right things under pressure.

In all walks of life we admire good leadership, talent, success, and the personal power associated with them. It is very American to value such things, and let's thank God that we live in a free nation where individual achievement is still honored and rewarded. May we never forget that the source of America's prosperity and influence is our freedom and that the source of our freedom is the word of God.

> *John 8:32, 36 – And you shall know the truth, and the truth shall make you free ... So if the Son sets you free, you will be free indeed.*

> *Gal. 5:1 – It was for freedom that Christ set us free ...*

> *2 Cor. 3:17 – ... where the Spirit of the Lord is, there is freedom.*

While we are impressed with all the human achievement and personal power operating out there in cosmos diabolicus (the Devil's world), God is not at all impressed with human achievement and power. To impress God requires making good decisions under the direction of the Holy Spirit. That's why David was said to be "the apple of God's eye" in Psalms 17:8. And that is why Stephen, whose courage in death was spectacular, received a standing ovation from Jesus Christ Himself in Acts 7:55. The death of Stephen is the only occasion where it is recorded that Christ *stood up* in the Throne Room. Because David and Stephen did not rely on human power, genius, or talent, they are a reminder that the Spirit-Directed Life is totally dependent upon the utilization of a supernatural power.

David made it clear that the source of his power was supernatural when he begged God not to remove the Holy Spirit from him after his greatest failure, "Operation Bathsheba":

> *Psalms 51:11 – Do not cast me away from Your presence, and do not take Your Holy Spirit from me.*

Here we have the slayer of Goliath, one of the Old Testament's greatest heroes and by far Israel's greatest king, reminding us that the source of his achievements was the power of the Holy Spirit. Prior to Operation Bathsheba, David had been out of fellowship with God for months for failure to go to war against Israel's enemies. At the very peak of his human power as King, David decided to take a vacation from his spiritual power. Being out of fellowship with God for failure to lead his army in battle, he had lost the power of the Holy Spirit temporarily and was in danger of losing it permanently.

Please be advised that the Spirit power that David and others had in the Old Testament was called "enduement." It was a limited empowerment of the Spirit given by God to certain individuals for a limited time and specific purpose (Ps. 51:11–12, Micah 3:8, Zech. 4:6). The Old Testament believers did not have the same Spirit empowerment available to Church Age believers, because Christ's strategic victory on the cross, His resurrection, and consequent seating at the right hand of the Father had not yet occurred.

> *John 7:39 – … for the Spirit was not yet given, because Jesus was not yet glorified.*

However, David was smart enough to know that he was dead in the water without the Old Testament limited empowerment of the Holy Spirit. David had just committed his greatest sin, and he knew that something specific was absolutely required before fellowship with God and the consequent empowerment of the Spirit could be restored. David knew exactly what he needed to do to recover fellowship and empowerment, and he did it.

> *Psalms 32:1–5, 11 – How blessed is he whose transgression is forgiven, whose sin is covered ... when I kept silent about my sin, my body wasted away through my groaning all day long [Groan Zone], for day and night Your hand was heavy upon me [Divine discipline], my vitality was drained away as with the fever-heat of summer; I acknowledged my sin to you, and my iniquity I did not hide; I said "I will confess my transgressions to the Lord"; and You forgave the guilt of my sin. Be glad in the Lord and rejoice you righteous ones [restored to the Power Zone], and shout for joy all you who are upright in heart.*

> *Gal. 5:22–23 – For the fruit of the Spirit is love, joy, peace, patience, kindness, goodness, faithfulness, gentleness, self-control ...*

Are you aware that what was required for a sinful David to be restored to fellowship with God is also required of us after we sin? David just told us what that required action is: it is confession of our own sins directly to God.

If you read chapter 1 of this book and studied diagram 3, you have already been introduced to the importance of confession of sin. If you did not read the first chapter, please do so now. This book is designed to be read in order; understanding the chapter you are reading is based on understanding previous chapters.

Why are Church Age believers free to confess their sins directly to God without going through ritual or an intermediary person such as a priest? It's very simple: all Church Age believers are priests. When Christ died for our sins on the cross and the temple veil was split (Mk. 15: 38), it opened the door to universal priesthood for the Church Age believer.

> *1 Pet. 2:5, 9 – ... you also as living stones are being built up as a spiritual house for a holy priesthood ... But you are a chosen race, a royal priesthood, a holy nation, a people for God's own possession ...*
>
> *Rev. 1:6 – ... and He has made us to be a kingdom, priests to His God and Father ...*

It is precisely because Church Age believers are all "priests" that we can pray with confidence about forgiveness of sins.

> *Heb. 4:16 – Let us therefore come boldly before the throne of grace ...*

I will address the issue of confession of sin in greater detail in the following chapters, but right now it is important to remember that confession is God's grace provision for getting us back under the Spirit's power.

Coining the Phrase "the Power Zone"

A reminder from chapter 1: the Christian life is a supernatural way of life. As such, it demands a supernatural power of execution. The supernatural power of execution for the Christian life is none other than the Holy Spirit.

We can live the Christian life only through the power of the Spirit. When we are empowered by the Spirit, we are living inside of a grace-provided sphere that I call the Power Zone. I coined this phrase because of numerous passages but particularly Eph. 3:16 and 2 Tim. 1:7:

... become strong by means of His power through His Spirit in the inner man. For God has not given us a Spirit of fear but of power ...

The Power Zone is the only position from which the Holy Spirit can control our life. If we are ever going to live the Spirit-Directed Life, the Apostle Paul tells us where the power will come from:

Rom. 15:13, 18–19 – ... that you may abound in hope through the power of the Holy Spirit. For I will not presume to speak of anything except what Christ has accomplished through me ... in the power of the Spirit.

1 Cor. 2:4–5 – And my message and my preaching were not in persuasive words of wisdom, but in demonstration of the Spirit and of power, that your faith should not rest on the wisdom of men but on the power of God.

When the Spirit controls our life, we have the magic touch, we consistently make the right decisions, and we have the power to grow spiritually and protect our spiritual advances. In short, when we are living the Spirit-Directed Life, it is because we are living in the Power Zone, under the power of God the Holy Spirit, courtesy of the grace of God.

The Origin of the Power Zone

Are you aware that God designed the Power Zone specifically for the earthly ministry of Jesus Christ?

Mt. 12:18 – Behold My Servant whom I have chosen; My Beloved in whom My soul is well pleased; I will put My Spirit upon Him ...

John 3:34; Col. 1:19 – For He whom God has sent speaks the words of God; for He gives the Spirit without measure. For it was the Father's good pleasure for all the fullness to dwell in Him.

Are you aware that most of what Christ accomplished during His earthly ministry was done in His Humanity, through the power of the Spirit, by living inside the Power Zone?

Luke 4:18 – The Spirit of the Lord is upon Me ...

Eph. 1:19–20 – And what is the surpassing greatness of His power toward us who believe. These are according to the standard of His inner power which has been made available in Christ ...

Christ's inner power, the Holy Spirit, has been made available to us. Diagram 1 should bring the above passages into perspective, along with the other passages listed to explain the origin of the Power Zone.

DIAGRAM 1: Origin of *"The Power Zone"*

CHRIST'S EARTHLY MINISTRY	CHRIST'S DEATH, RESURRECTION, ASCENSION
LIVED *THE POWER ZONE* FOR US	MADE *THE POWER ZONE* AVAILABLE TO US
*Eph. 1:19...*according to the standard of His inner power...	*Eph. 1:20...*which has been made available in Christ, when He raised Him from the dead, and seated Him at His right hand in the heavenly places...
Matt. 12:18; Lk. 4:18; Jn. 3:34; Col. 1:19	*Jn. 4:23-24; 7:39; 14:17, 26; 16:7, 13-14; Acts 1:8; Heb. 9:14; Eph. 5:18*

Through the power of the Holy Spirit, Christ lived inside the Power Zone during His earthly ministry. Because of His death, resurrection, and ascension to the right hand of the Father, He made the Power Zone available to you and me.

Are you aware that during the last three hours of the cross, the Father and the Spirit could not have fellowship with the Son because He was made sin for us?

> *2 Cor. 5:21; Mt. 27:46 – For He made Him who knew*
> *no sin to become sin for us ...*
> *"My God, My God, why have You forsaken Me?"*
> *[loss of fellowship]*

Are you aware that if the Spirit could not have fellowship with Christ because He was made sin for us, that the Spirit likewise cannot have fellowship with us when we become spiritually dead through sin?

> *Rom, 6:23; James 1:15, 2:26 – For the wages of sin*
> *is death ... when sin is accomplished, it brings forth*
> *death ... the body without the Spirit is dead ...*

Are you aware that the last thing Christ said to the Disciples before He ascended to the Father was that He was leaving the Spirit (the Power Zone) behind for all Church Age believers?

> *Acts 1:8 – ... but you shall receive power when the*
> *Holy Spirit has come upon you.*

Since the Power Zone was the last thing Christ mentioned to the disciples prior to His ascension, do you think that the power of the Spirit just might have something to do with how we live our Christian life?

Are you aware that the very same Power Zone of the Spirit that the Father gave to Christ to sustain Him throughout His earthly ministry is the identical Power Zone that Christ has conferred to you and me?

> *John 15:16; Eph. 6:10 – You have not chosen me, but*
> *I have chosen you and appointed [tithemi = placed*
> *inside the Power Zone] you so that you may advance*

and produce fruit. In the future, keep on becoming empowered by means of His conferred power.

John 16:7, 13–14 – ... it is to your advantage that I go away; for if I do not go away, the Helper shall not come to you; but if I go, I will send Him to you ... But when He, the Spirit of truth, comes, He will guide you into all the truth; for He will not speak on His own initiative, but whatever he hears He will speak; and He will disclose to you what is to come. He shall glorify Me ... shall take of Mine and disclose it to you.

Gal. 4:6 – And because you are sons, God has sent forth the Spirit of His Son into our hearts ...

Eph. 3:20 – Now to the One having the power far beyond all things to do infinitely more than we could ask or imagine, according to the power that is effective in us.

Are you aware that the Power Zone that Christ conferred to me and you at the moment of our salvation is the only power by which we can serve God?

1 Tim. 1:12 – I thank Christ Jesus our Lord, who has empowered me ... putting me into Service.

Rom. 7:6 – ... serve in newness of the Spirit ...

Rom. 8:14 – For all who are being led by the Spirit of God, these are the sons of God.

Are you aware that to be led by the Spirit of God requires becoming empowered by the Spirit again and again and again throughout our lives?

Eph. 6:10 – ... keep on becoming empowered ...

The empowerment of the Spirit is to be recurring. It must be done again and again. Why? Because we lose the empowerment of the Spirit through sin, and we sin daily. Notice also that when we combine the last phrases of Eph. 6:10 and 3:20, and 1 Tim. 1:12, it makes it even clearer that the Power Zone was conferred to us by Christ Himself:

> *... empowered by means of His conferred power ... according to the power that is effective in us ... Christ Jesus ... who has empowered me ... putting me into service*

When you combine those phrases with Acts 1:8—*you shall receive power when the Holy Spirit has come upon you*—several things should become obvious:

1. The Power Zone is a gift from Jesus Christ to every Church Age believer.
2. The Power Zone is supernatural.
3. The Power Zone is effective.
4. The Power Zone is our only source of power to execute the Christian life.
5. The Power Zone is a command; God commands us to live under the Spirit's power:

> *Gal. 4:6 – And because you are sons, God has sent forth the Spirit of His Son into our hearts ...*

> *1 John 2:6 – The one who says he abides in Him ought himself to walk in the same manner as He walked.*

> *Eph. 3:16 – ... become strong by means of His power through His Spirit ...*

An Unprecedented Power System

Are you aware that because Christ left His very own Power Zone to Church Age believers that we have the most unique power system ever made available to man?

> *Eph. 3:2–5, 9, 16–20 – If indeed you have heard of the dispensation of God's grace which was given to me for you ... that by revelation there was made known to me ... the mystery of Christ, which in other dispensations was not made known to the sons of men as it has now been revealed to His holy apostles and prophets in the Spirit ... and to bring to light what is the dispensation of the mystery, which for dispensations has been hidden in God ... that He would grant you, according to the riches of His glory, to be empowered through His Spirit in the inner man; so that Christ may dwell in your hearts through faith; and that you, being rooted and grounded in love, may be able to comprehend with all believers what is the breadth, length, height and depth, and to know the love of Christ which surpasses knowledge, that you may be filled up to all the fullness of God ... according to the power that works within us.*

Paul is telling us here that there was a unique body of knowledge hidden in God to all previous dispensations of humanity; that this mystery doctrine revealed a unique Church Age dispensation in which the power of the Spirit would be given to all believers by Christ; that the Spirit's power was the power through which Christ Himself lived; that the quality of this power is unprecedented in human history; and that Christ's very own power zone is now available to you and me.

The Eph. 3 verses represent one of the most profound references to the power of the Spirit available to us anywhere in scripture. The "breadth ... depth" verse refers specifically to the compartments of the *human* spirit, which is the target of the teaching ministry of the Holy Spirit. Why is that important? Because the teaching ministry of the Holy Spirit is only operational when we are inside the Power Zone. Not only that, but when we lose the power of the Spirit because of sin, all ministries of the Spirit in our personal life are shut down. Who shuts them down? We do, through sin, and it is sin that causes our temporary spiritual death.

> *Eph. 4:30; 1 Thes. 5:19; Jm. 1:15, 2:26 – ... do not grieve the Holy Spirit ... do not quench the Holy Spirit ... sin, when accomplished, brings forth death ... the body without the Spirit is dead.*

Are you aware that the unprecedented availability of the Spirit's control of our life through the Power Zone is a major part of the new covenant to Church Age believers made available by Jesus Christ?

> *2 Cor. 3:5–6 – ... our adequacy is from God, who also made us adequate as servants of a new covenant, not of the letter, but of the Spirit; for the letter kills, but the Spirit gives life.*

> *Rom. 8:2 – For the law of the Spirit of life in Christ Jesus has set you free ...*

> *2 Cor. 5:17 – Therefore if anyone is in Christ [Security Zone], he is a new creature; the old things [the Mosaic Law] passed away; behold, new things [Power Zone doctrines] have come.*

> *Heb. 8:6; 11:40 – But now He has obtained a more excellent ministry, by as much as He is also the mediator of a better covenant [Church Age mystery doctrines] which has been enacted on better promises ... because God had provided something better for us.*

Are you aware that the mystery of the universal availability of the Power Zone was so completely hidden by God until the Church Age that not even the angels were aware of it?

> *1 Pet. 1:12 – ... these things which now have been announced to you through those who preached the gospel to you by the Holy Spirit sent from heaven – things the angels long to look into.*

> *Eph. 3:10 – ... in order that the manifold wisdom of God might now be made known through the church to the rulers and the authorities in the heavenly places.*

Are you aware that the availability of the Power Zone to Church Age believers is so important that staying inside the Power Zone is a major issue from the book of Acts to Revelation?

> *Acts 1:8 – ... you shall receive power when the Holy Spirit has come upon you.*

> *Rev. 3:19–20 – "Those whom I love, I reprove and discipline; be diligent therefore, and repent; Behold I stand at the door and knock; if anyone hears My voice and opens the door, I will come in to him and will dine with him and he with Me."*

Some may be shocked to realize that Rev. 3:19–20 is not a salvation passage; it is a passage reminding the believer who is out of fellowship to get back inside the Power Zone by "opening the door," a metaphor for recovering fellowship with God by confessing sin. We are required to confess our sins just as David was.

The supernatural power of the Holy Spirit is so critical to Church Age believers that verse 22 of Rev. 3 reminds us once again to stay inside the Power Zone so that we can hear the Spirit's message:

> *Rev. 3:22 – "He who has an ear, let him hear what the Spirit says to the churches."*

The phrase "what the Spirit says to the churches" places the focus on the teaching ministry of the Spirit, which only occurs inside the Power Zone. When we are out of fellowship with God through sin—in other words, outside the Power Zone—the teaching ministry of the Spirit is shut down. Paul makes this clear in 1 Cor. 3, where being out of fellowship with God is called being "fleshly":

> *1 Cor. 3:1–3 – And I, believers, could not speak to you as to spiritual men, but as to men of flesh, as to babes in Christ. I gave you milk to drink, not solid food; for you were not yet able to receive it. Indeed, even now you are not yet able, for you are still fleshly. For since there is jealousy and strife among you, are you not fleshly, and are you not walking like mere men?*

The phrase "walking like mere men" is very important; it means we are outside the Power Zone, imitating the unbeliever. By doing so, we have cloned ourselves under our previous power source, our old sin nature. We will take up in detail the major issue of "cloning ourselves" in Chapter 6, "The Clone Zone."

Our Two Relationships with God

Prior to reading chapter 1, were you aware that at the moment of salvation, God placed us into two different relationships with Him, one permanent and one temporary?

> *Gal. 5:25 – If we live by the Spirit, let us also walk by the Spirit.*

In Gal. 5:25, "live" refers to a permanent relationship with the Spirit, but "walk" refers to a temporary relationship. The permanent relationship refers to the indwelling of the Spirit in the Security Zone, and the temporary relationship refers to being empowered by the Spirit in the Power Zone. Diagram 2 should help explain these simple but very important differences.

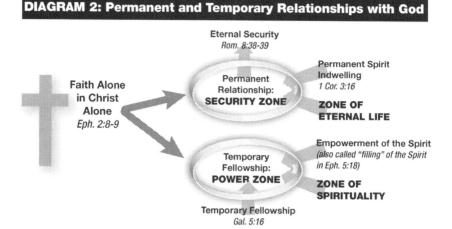

DIAGRAM 2: Permanent and Temporary Relationships with God

You will notice in diagram 2 that we have two relationships with God, one permanent and one temporary. The top circle is about eternal security (i.e., the Security Zone). Be assured that when we believe in Christ, we cannot lose our salvation. We cannot get out of the top circle.

> *Rom. 8:38–39 – For I am persuaded that neither death, nor life, nor angels, nor principalities, nor things present, nor things to come, nor powers, nor height, nor depth, nor any other created thing, shall be able to separate us from the love of God, which is in Christ Jesus our Lord.*

The top circle represents our permanent union with Christ, referred to in the Bible as being "in Christ." Being in permanent union with Christ means there is no way we can ever lose our salvation. Besides Rom. 8:38–39, other references to eternal security include John 10:28, 1 John 5:11–12, and Isaiah 43:1.

The bottom circle represents our temporary fellowship with God inside the Power Zone, described in scripture in varying ways:

- *filled with the Spirit,* Eph. 5:18
- *walk in Him,* Col. 2:6

- *walk in the Spirit,* Gal. 5:16
- *walk as children of light,* Eph. 5:8
- *walk in the light,* 1 Jn. 1:7
- *abide in Him,* 1 Jn. 2:27
- *abide in Me,* Jn. 15:4
- *he who abides in Me,* Jn. 15:5
- *If you abide in Me,* Jn. 15:7
- *abide in His love,* Jn. 15:10

A good illustration of the difference between the indwelling and the empowerment of the Spirit in the top and bottom circles is to think of the relationship between parents and children. Children and parents do not always get along, but they are inseparably and forever related. A child disobeying parents is like the believer out of the Power Zone—temporary fellowship is lost, but there is still a permanent relationship. A believer out of fellowship with God due to un-confessed sin is no longer empowered by the Spirit, because the Spirit has been grieved (Eph. 4:30) and possibly quenched (1 Thes. 5:19). However, that same believer is still indwelled by the Spirit, because the indwelling means there is a permanent relationship.

It is important to remember from diagram 2 that the indwelling of the Spirit occurs in the top circle, the Security Zone, while the empowerment of the Spirit occurs in the bottom circle, the Power Zone. I saw the diagram of the top and bottom circles for the first time under the incomparable ministry of Col. R. B. Thieme, and only then did I realize what the Christian life was all about: the Christian life can only be lived inside the bottom circle ... inside the Power Zone, under the direction of the Spirit!

Although I had been a believer since junior high school, spiritual matters had never really fallen into place for me until I was well into my early twenties. The top and bottom circles did it for me— the lights came on! Before you finish this book, I hope the lights will come on for you. Since most of this book is about the bottom circle, you may be several chapters into this book before you begin to realize the full implications of diagram 2. Hang in there, and you will begin to see the importance of the bottom circle, the Power Zone.

It is of great importance to distinguish between the indwelling of the Spirit in the top circle and the empowerment of the Spirit in the bottom circle. Why is this so critical? Because we are never commanded to be indwelled by the Spirit—we can't lose the indwelling—but we are commanded repeatedly in the New Testament to be empowered by the Spirit because we can, we do, and we will lose the empowerment. We lose it through sin, and we sin daily.

If believers don't know the difference between the indwelling of the Spirit in the top circle and the empowerment of the Spirit in the bottom circle, they'll never understand the Power Zone.

1. The Power Zone exists only for Church Age believers.
2. The Power Zone is available only because Christ lived inside of it, then gave it to us.
3. The Power Zone is temporary, because we cannot completely avoid sin.
4. The Power Zone is available to us only through confession of sin.
5. The Power Zone is the only way possible to live the Spirit-Directed Life.

The Competing Power Zone Called "the Flesh"

> *Gal. 5:16–17 – ... walk by the Spirit, and you will not carry out the desire of the flesh. For the flesh sets its desire against the Spirit, and the Spirit against the flesh; for these are in opposition to one another, so that you can't do the things that you please.*

> *John 15:5 – ... he who abides in Me (Power Zone) ... bears much fruit; for apart from Me you can do nothing.*

Rom. 8:5 – For those who are according to the flesh set their minds on the things of the flesh [out of the Power Zone], but those who are according to the Spirit, the things of the Spirit [in the Power Zone].

The phrases "according to the flesh" and "according to the Spirit" refer to our soul status at any given moment after salvation. Our soul status is that we are either out of fellowship with God or we are in fellowship with God. We're either out of the Power Zone, or we're in the Power Zone.

Are you aware that "the flesh" refers to our still-resident sin nature, and when we commit sin, we become spiritually dead?

James 1:15 – ... for when sin is accomplished, it brings forth death.

James 2:26 – ... the body without the Spirit is dead ...

Rom. 8:6a – For the mind set on the flesh is death ...

In other words, sin puts us outside the Power Zone. Diagram 3 should help explain.

DIAGRAM 3: Sin Causes Loss of Empowerment but Not Indwelling

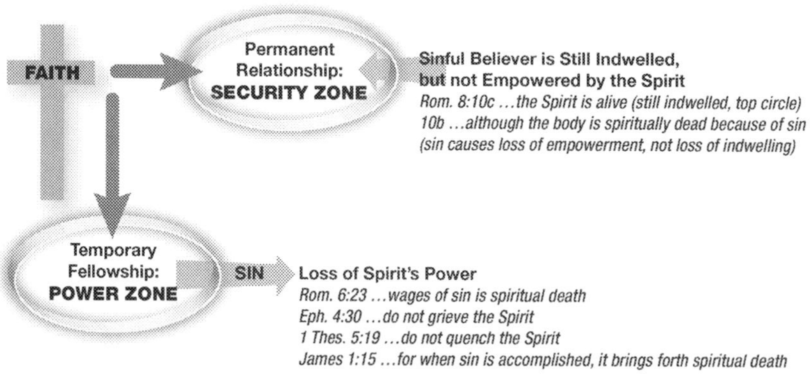

FAITH

Permanent Relationship:
SECURITY ZONE

Sinful Believer is Still Indwelled,
but not Empowered by the Spirit
Rom. 8:10c ...the Spirit is alive (still indwelled, top circle)
10b ...although the body is spiritually dead because of sin
(sin causes loss of empowerment, not loss of indwelling)

Temporary Fellowship:
POWER ZONE

SIN

Loss of Spirit's Power
Rom. 6:23 ...wages of sin is spiritual death
Eph. 4:30 ...do not grieve the Spirit
1 Thes. 5:19 ...do not quench the Spirit
James 1:15 ...for when sin is accomplished, it brings forth spiritual death

In diagram 3, Romans 8:10 is an important verse. It tells us that we never lose the indwelling of the Spirit in the top circle, but that sin causes the loss of empowerment of the Spirit in the bottom circle because God cannot have fellowship with a sinner. In other words, sin never gets us out of the Security Zone, but sin always gets us out of the Power Zone. Sin causes loss of fellowship, not loss of salvation. Think of it this way: there is one Lord, one faith, one baptism (Security Zone), but many empowerments (Power Zone) through confession of sin.

Notice in diagram 3 that sin grieves and quenches the Holy Spirit, making us spiritually dead, and the empowerment of the Spirit is lost. Depending upon the believer's attitude toward God and toward sin, loss of empowerment can be brief, prolonged, or in some extreme cases permanent, if the believer refuses to confess sins.

It should be obvious that once we are out of fellowship with God and out of the Power Zone because of personal sin, there's no way we can get back in fellowship with God unless the grace of God provides a way to re-enter the Power Zone. We must do exactly what David did to recover fellowship: confess sins directly to God.

Psalms 32:3, 5 – When I kept silent about my sin,
my body wasted away through my groaning all day

long [Groan Zone]. I acknowledged my sin to You, and my iniquity I did not hide; I said "I will confess my transgressions to the Lord"; And You forgave the guilt of my sin.

1 John 1:9 – If we confess our sins, He is faithful and righteous to forgive us our sins and to cleanse us from all unrighteousness.

Rom. 8:6b – ... but the mind set on the Spirit is life and peace.

John 6:63 – It is the Spirit that gives life, the flesh profits nothing.

Are you becoming aware that the Power Zone, which Christ gave to you and me, is the only means of soul-control for living the Spirit-Directed Life?

2 Tim. 1:7 – For God has not given us a Spirit of fear, but of power, and of love, and of a stabilized mind.

In the Galatians and Romans verses at the beginning of this section, the term "the flesh" refers to our resident sin nature. That term should tip off any average Bible student that there is a competing power zone that can totally control our soul. The flesh, as the competing power zone, constantly battles the Spirit for soul-control. We will take up the issue of spiritual warfare in more detail later on. Diagram 3 should make it clear that when we recover from sin through God's grace provision of confession, we are cleansed from sin, we are reinstated into the Power Zone, we are back under the control of the Spirit, and therefore we are spiritually alive.

The 2 Tim. 1:7 passage should elicit the personal question "Am I walking in fear or in power?" Fear is from our sin nature; power is from the Spirit. In your Christian life, are you doing the "wimp walk" or the "power walk"?

In the game of football, the "power position" is the body position from which you can stop the advance of an opposing player. In basketball, there is that "sweet spot" from which a player can't miss a shot. In baseball, the pitcher is said to have "the right stuff" when he can put the right pitch in the right spot at the right speed. In track and field, pole-vaulters experience power when their combined approach, plant, and swing triggers the kinetic power in the pole to launch them over the bar.

The Spirit-Directed Life is like the power position, the sweet spot, having the right stuff, and learning how to use the power in the pole. The power of the Spirit is always available simply by naming our sins.

Let's summarize what I hope you have seen so far in chapter 2:

1. In Christianity, God provides the Power Zone in which the Holy Spirit empowers soul-control so that every believer in Christ can live the Spirit-Directed Life.
2. However, there is a competing power zone constantly residing inside of us that fights against the Spirit for soul-control. This competing power zone is called the sin nature or the flesh, and it is the source of sin.
3. The grace of God has made available to every believer the grace provision of confession of sin so that we may return to the Power Zone and resume the Spirit-Directed Life.

Are you aware that it is being empowered by the Spirit in the bottom circle that makes us spiritual, and not the indwelling of the Spirit in the top circle?

> *Rom. 8:10 – And if Christ in you, though the body is spiritually dead because of sin [no spirit empowerment] yet the Spirit is alive because of righteousness [Spirit still indwells because God's righteousness was given to us permanently at salvation, Phil. 3:9].*

At this point we should all ask ourselves this question: "Who is directing our life, the Spirit or the flesh?" You've probably seen the bumper sticker that says "If God is your co-pilot, change seats!" How true that is! Either our sin nature is in charge, or the Spirit is in charge, and we choose our pilot every day, moment by moment.

Are you aware that the only pilot that allows us to travel first class through the Christian life is the Holy Spirit, who was given to us by Christ?

> *John 10:10 – I came that they might have life, and have it more abundantly.*
>
> *John 16:7 – ... if I do not go away, the Helper shall not come to you; but if I go, I will send Him to you.*
>
> *Acts 1:8 – ... you will receive power when the Holy Spirit has come upon you ...*
>
> *John 14:26 – ... He will teach you all things and bring to remembrance all things that I said to you.*
>
> *Gal. 5:22–23 – But the fruit of the Spirit is love, joy, peace, patience, kindness, goodness, faithfulness, gentleness, self-control.*

Defining Spirituality and Carnality

When we are under the Spirit's power, we are said to be "spiritual." When we are under the power of our sin nature we are said to be "carnal." This brings us to the all-important definitions of what these two terms mean.

- Spirituality is absolute soul-control by the Holy Spirit.
- Carnality is absolute soul-control by our sin nature.

It's just that simple! Spirituality is the absolute state of soul where we receive power, inspiration, and direction from the Spirit. Spirituality is living inside the Power Zone, in fellowship with God, in the bottom circle.

Carnality is the absolute state of soul where we receive energy, motivation, and direction from our sin nature. Carnality is living in the competing power zones, out of fellowship with God, outside the bottom circle.

Spirituality is provided entirely by the grace of God, through confession of sin. Carnality is entirely the work of weakness from within. Therefore, spirituality is by grace, and carnality is by the works of our sin nature.

Spirituality does not come in degrees like spiritual maturity. Spiritual maturity is a relative state of soul, dependent upon the amount of Bible doctrine resident in the human spirit. But spirituality is an absolute state of soul, dependent upon our use of the grace provision, the confession of sin. By now you should be aware that only confession of sin gets us back into the Power Zone of Spirit control after we have been living in the competing power zone of the sin nature.

Many Christians remain unaware of how to get back into fellowship with God after sin. Imagine living your entire Christian life being perpetually "unclean and unaware"—in other words, being out of fellowship with God because of sin, and being unaware of the need for confession. Awareness is the first step in getting back in fellowship with God after sin.

Failure to understand how to access the Power Zone means that many Christians today are simply attending church and living out the warning of 2 Tim. 3:5 ...

> *Holding to a form of godliness, although they have denied its power ...*

Many churches are only teaching the results of spirituality and then expecting their congregations to go out and execute the Christian life through the energy of the flesh. It can't be done! We are commanded to accomplish supernatural things that can be accomplished only inside the Power Zone. For example,

> *John 15:12 – This is My commandment, that you love one another, just as I have loved you.*

Do we really believe that we can love other believers as Christ loves us without knowing how to access the power of the Spirit? It's as futile as a pole-vaulting coach handing the pole to an athlete who has never vaulted and telling him nothing more than "use this pole and clear that bar." Talk about a disaster waiting to happen! It's as futile as a church covering the passages on "the fruits of the Spirit," but never teaching how to recover from sin and get back into the Power Zone where the fruits of the Spirit are produced (diagram 4). It's as ridiculous as teaching the importance of prayer but failing to teach getting back into fellowship with God by confessing sin prior to prayer so that prayer can be heard (Chapter 4, diagram 5, "Why Confess Sin Prior to Prayer?").

Let me briefly return to the illustration of the pole-vaulter. Vaulters experience an exciting ride when their combined approach, plant, and swing triggers the kinetic power in the pole to launch them over the bar. There is power in the vaulter's pole, but the vaulter must know how to access that power. There is power in the Spirit, but you have to know how to access the Spirit's power. And it's so simple that you should wonder why it is so seldom taught—and when it is taught, why the dots are not being connected between confession of sin and producing the fruits of the Spirit. Believers need to understand how to go from carnality back to spirituality, as in diagram 4:

DIAGRAM 4: Spiritual Life Versus Spiritual Death

Believer Out Of Fellowship –
Spiritually Dead
Rom. 6:23 ...wages of sin is spiritual death
Eph. 4:30 ...do not grieve the Spirit
1 Thes. 5:19 ...do not quench the Spirit
James 1:15 ...for when sin is accomplished, it brings forth spiritual death

Believer Restored To Fellowship –
Spiritually Alive
Rom. 8:2 ...the Spirit of life has set you free from the law of sin and death
Rom. 8:6 ...the mind set on the Spirit is life
Rom. 8:13 ...if by the Spirit you are putting to death the deeds of the body, you will live
2 Cor. 3:6 ...the Spirit gives life

Diagram 4 should help you see how simple it is to get back into the Power Zone after sin. We get back into fellowship with God by confession of sin. It's just that simple!

Why did God make recovery of fellowship so simple? One reason is that we all begin the Christian life as spiritual morons. Spiritual morons require simplicity. To recover fellowship with God after sin requires something simple, not some system of ritual or penance or guilt. We will cover other reasons in a later chapter and will look at more documentation from scripture, but for now, just remember that recovery of fellowship with God after sin is by grace. By grace we were placed into permanent union with Christ at salvation. Because Christ did all the work and we are in union with Him, the Father can only honor Christ's work in dying for our sins and restore us to fellowship simply through the grace provision of confession of sin. Confession is not a license to sin; it restores the power to serve.

Are you becoming aware that at any given moment after salvation we are either 100 percent empowered by the Spirit and therefore spiritual, or we are 100 percent empowered by our sin nature and therefore carnal?

Rom. 8:13 – For if you are living according to the flesh, you must die [die spiritually due to sin]; but if by the Spirit ... you will live [live spiritually in the Power Zone after confession].

What verse 13 and much of Romans chapter 8 is telling us is that at any given moment after salvation, we are either 100 percent spiritual or 100 percent carnal. We will cover the issue of soul-status being either spiritual or carnal in more detail in another chapter.

When we are out of fellowship with God, we are in one of four spiritual death zones empowered by our sin nature. "Zones" is plural, because although "the flesh" is singular in scripture, there are varying degrees of sinfulness outside the Power Zone. We will cover these varying degrees of sinfulness with scripture references in the progression of this book, but for now, diagram 5 emphasizes how involved sin can be. Diagram 5 of this chapter is like diagram 4 from chapter 1. Again, diagrams and scripture references will be repeated throughout this book, since repetition enhances learning.

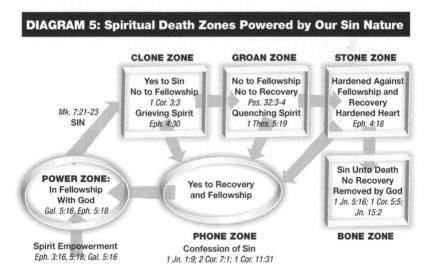

DIAGRAM 5: Spiritual Death Zones Powered by Our Sin Nature

Obviously, being controlled by the Spirit inside the Power Zone is the key to the spiritual life. But before we get too far into the Power Zone it is necessary to see why the Father first invented the Power Zone for the humanity of Christ, and then how Christ made it available to all Church Age believers. All three members of the Trinity have accomplished awesome things to make the Power Zone available to us. We will examine these awesome things in Chapter 3, "From Spiritual Death to Security and Power."

CHAPTER 2 KEY POINTS

- Church Age believers are free to confess sins directly to God because the cross removed the barrier between God and man. (p. 20)
- God designed the Power Zone specifically for the earthly ministry of Jesus Christ. (p. 21)
- The Power Zone is: a gift from Christ; supernatural; effective; our source of power; a command. (p. 25)
- "Walking like mere men" means we are out of the Power Zone, imitating the unbeliever. (p. 29)
- Being controlled by the Spirit inside the Power Zone is the key to the Spirit-Directed Life. (p. 41)

CHAPTER 3: FROM SPIRITUAL DEATH TO SECURITY AND POWER

If we are to have a relationship with God the Father, we have to make a decision about God's Son, Jesus Christ. The Christian life requires constant decision-making. Once we are saved by faith alone in Christ alone, we have to make daily decisions about recovery from sin. In both cases—salvation and post-salvation recovery from sin—only the grace of God provides the means to change our status from spiritual death to spiritual life.

In this chapter, we're going to look at five very important things:

1. Physical birth in relationship to spiritual death. It is important for us to understand that physical birth caused us to be born spiritually dead. But it's even more important to understand that after salvation, although we are still saved, sin also causes us to become spiritually dead, which means separation from God with regard to fellowship.

2. Acquiring the Holy Spirit – God gave us the Holy Spirit at the moment of salvation for at least five essential reasons:

- Fellowship with Him
- Empowerment
- Spiritual growth
- Production
- Effective prayer

3. Acquiring our human spirit and understanding its purpose. This is important because our human spirit is the foundation of

the spiritual house inside our soul and therefore represents our spiritual I.Q.

4. The grace bypass of human I.Q. It is important and reassuring to realize that the grace of God will not allow human genetics to limit our spiritual growth.

5. The ultimate implant. It is important and reassuring to know that because the indwelling of the Spirit is permanent, it gives us the opportunity and privilege of being empowered by the Spirit so that we can carry out God's perfect plan for our lives.

Physical Birth in Relationship to Spiritual Death

Before we accepted Christ as savior, it was impossible for our soul to be empowered by anything other than our genetically inherited sin nature. The human race inherited the sin nature genetically from Adam and Eve. Let's go back to Genesis 2:17, where Adam and Eve committed the original sin:

> *... but from the tree of knowledge of good and evil you shall not eat, for in the day that you eat from it you will surely die.*

In the Hebrew, the verb for "die" (*mut*) is doubled, meaning two deaths, one immediate and the other distant. The immediate death is spiritual, and the distant death is physical. After eating from the tree, Adam and Eve died spiritually immediately but would not die physically for hundreds of years. When we translate Gen. 2:17 into modern English, it reads like this:

> *In the day you eat from the tree, dying spiritually, you will eventually die physically.*

This is one of the most important verses in the Bible, because it tells us from the very beginning that sin causes *spiritual* death. In the Christian life it is spiritual, not physical, death that we need to be concerned with on a moment-by-moment basis. The New

Testament reminds us once again that the result of personal sin is spiritual death.

Romans 6:23 – For the wages of sin is death ...

The Greek word for death in Rom. 6:23 is *thanatos*, which means "the separation of man from God," or spiritual death. This means that any sin committed by a believer in Christ, regardless of the degree or the category of sin, immediately separates us spiritually from God. Both the Old and New Testaments make it very clear that personal sin results in spiritual death, a soul status that separates us from God.

Isaiah 59:2 – But your sins have made a separation between you and your God, and your sins have hid His face from you, so that He does not hear.

The moment we sin, we are out of fellowship with God. What does that mean? It means we are out of the Power Zone, out of the bottom circle, because sin made us spiritually dead to God. Common sense should tell us that spiritual death is the issue when we sin, not physical death, since we don't die physically when we sin. The whole point is this: when we become spiritually dead to God because of sin, only a grace provision from God can make us spiritually alive again and place us back in fellowship with Him.

Once Adam and Eve sinned in the Garden and acquired a "sin nature," spiritual death was inherited genetically at the point of physical birth by all of humankind:

1 Cor. 15:22 – In Adam all die.

It is important to understand that as unbelievers, we were all born with at least two things in common: we were born physically alive, but spiritually dead. Diagram 1 should help explain.

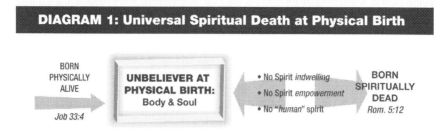

DIAGRAM 1: Universal Spiritual Death at Physical Birth

Although physical birth brought us physical life, it also brought us spiritual death. Therefore, spiritually speaking, we all have a third thing in common – we were all born in the same location: Spiritual Death Valley.

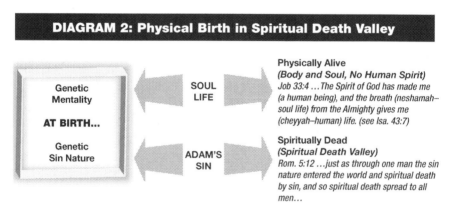

DIAGRAM 2: Physical Birth in Spiritual Death Valley

Job 33:4 and Romans 5:12 tell us that God assigned two things to our genetic makeup at physical birth: soul life to our mentality, and Adam's sin genetically to our sin nature. In Romans 5:12, the word for death once again is *thanatos*, meaning the separation of man from God—in other words, spiritual death. So as you can see in diagrams 1 and 2, there are at least five major problems at physical birth:

1. We are born under the control of our genetically inherited sin nature.
2. We are born spiritually dead, in Spiritual Death Valley.

3. We are born without the indwelling of the Holy Spirit, and therefore ...

4. We are born without the empowerment of the Spirit.

5. We are born without a human spirit (We can't understand, store, or apply God's word).

As unbelievers, there was no spiritual warfare possible between our sin nature and a non-resident Holy Spirit over who was going to control our soul. Our sin nature controlled us because it had no rivals, and the very best we could produce was "human good." God's word makes it very clear what the essence of our sin nature is. By categorizing verses, we get a clear picture in the following diagram.

DIAGRAM 3: The Four Categories of Sin Nature Production

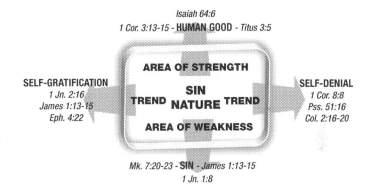

While there are many other passages describing our sin nature, the passages in diagram 3 help to establish the four categories of sin nature production. While we all have the same sin nature format as in diagram 3, no two people have exactly the same trends or exactly the same strengths and weaknesses. Therefore, everyone's sin nature is different. Once we begin to recognize that our sin nature has four different problem areas that compete against the Holy Spirit, it should become clear why the word of God says in Jer. 17: 9,

The heart is more deceitful than all else and is desperately sick ...

Acquiring the Holy Spirit

After the fall of man in the Garden, man was only capable of producing from the four areas of the sin nature. Since man can please God only from production empowered by the Spirit, the grace plan of God provided a way for man to get back under the Spirit's power. While spiritual death was obviously a problem for man, it wasn't for God. The sin nature is passed genetically only through the man because at the time of the original sin in the Garden, the man sinned *deliberately*. Since the woman was deceived into sinning, she does not pass the sin nature on genetically.

> *1 Tim. 2:14 – And it was not Adam who was deceived, but the woman being quite deceived, fell into transgression.*

You will notice in diagram 2 that Rom. 5:12 says that through one man the sin nature entered the world. It does not say "through one man and one woman." The sin nature is passed through the man since he sinned deliberately. The uniquely born God-man, Jesus Christ, was born without a sin nature due to Spirit conception. His Holiness, plus His ability to remain in the Power Zone, made Him qualified to bear the penalty of sinful man. The father of the Deity of Christ was God the Holy Spirit, not man. Therefore, Christ was born with without a sin nature but also with true human freewill. Our salvation was accomplished because Christ subordinated His own will to the Father's:

> *Mat. 26:39 – ... Father, if it is possible, let this cup [the cross] pass from me; nevertheless, not My will but Your will be done.*

> *John 19:30; Luke 23:46 – ... it is finished ... Father, into Your hands I dismiss My Spirit*

Although Satan is the great deceiver of man, he is not omniscient. The genius of Satan cannot compete with the omniscience of God.

Because Christ executed the Father's plan for salvation on the cross, humankind has the option of acquiring spiritual life through faith alone in Christ alone:

> *Eph. 2:8–9 – For by grace are you saved through faith; and that not of yourselves; it is the gift of God, not of works, lest any man should boast.*

> *Titus 3:5 – Not by works of righteousness which we have done, but according to His mercy He saved us, by the washing of regeneration and renewing by the Holy Spirit.*

> *John 3:16 – For God so loved the world that He gave His uniquely born Son, that whoever believes in Him should not perish, but have eternal life.*

Obviously, the term "uniquely born" (the correct translation instead of the more commonly translated "only begotten") refers to the virgin birth. The function of Mary in giving birth to Christ was to serve as the "true humanity" for the Spirit conception of our Savior. Through Spirit conception, true humanity plus undiminished Deity could be born in one person, Jesus Christ. Therefore, Mary is the mother of the humanity of Christ, nothing more and nothing less. To deify Mary is blasphemy, because she had a sin nature just like the rest of us. Diagram 4 demonstrates the effectiveness of the virgin birth and the spiritual rebirth of man through belief in Christ's taking our place on the cross.

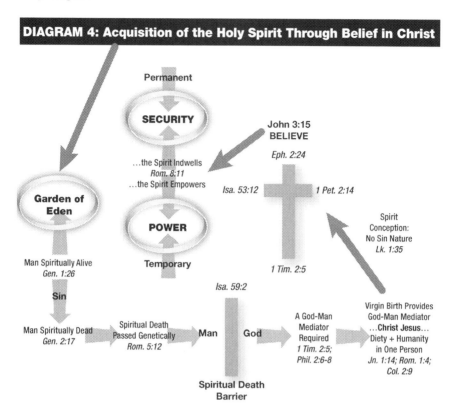

DIAGRAM 4: Acquisition of the Holy Spirit Through Belief in Christ

Diagram 4 should make it obvious that at the moment of salvation, faith alone in Christ alone, we are entered into the Security Zone and into the Power Zone simultaneously. Rom. 8:11–13 makes it clear that the indwelling and the empowerment of the Spirit are not the same thing. So does Gal. 5:25:

> *If we live by the Spirit [Security Zone], let us also*
> *walk by the Spirit [Power Zone].*

Why is this difference so important? Because failure to understand the difference between the Security Zone and the Power Zone means failure to understand spirituality in the Church Age. The Spiritual life is lived exclusively inside the Power Zone. While the Security Zone represents our position in Christ, the Power Zone represents our experience under the Spirit's control. As we will see in chapter 4, back-to-back verses in Romans 8 make it clear that at any given moment after salvation, we are either spiritual or we are carnal. Gal. 5:16–17 also makes this essential doctrine clear:

> *But I say, walk by the Spirit [Power Zone] and you will not carry out the desire of the flesh. For the flesh sets its desire against the Spirit, and the Spirit against the flesh; for these are in opposition to one another, so that you may not do the things that you please.*

When we contrast 1 Cor. 3:3 with Eph. 5:1, again it is clear that either we are imitating the unbeliever outside the Power Zone, or we are imitating Christ inside the Power Zone:

> *... are you not fleshly ... walking like mere men? ... be imitators of God ...*

Either we are spiritual inside the Power Zone, or we are carnal outside the Power Zone. If we are inside the Power Zone, we are spiritually alive. If we are outside the Power Zone, we are spiritually dead. Again, failure to understand this means failure to understand spirituality in the Church Age. The failure to understand spirituality sentences the believer to a futile attempt at the Christian life under the energy of the flesh (sin nature).

From the moment of salvation, our body is always a temple of the Holy Spirit, which refers to the indwelling of the Spirit in the top circle—the Security Zone—in diagram 4. Keep in mind that we can never get out of the top circle, which is why I named it the Security Zone. But since sin defiles the temple, the moment we sin, we lose the empowerment of the Spirit, because we are out of the bottom circle, the Power Zone. Remember that when Rom. 6:23 tells us "the wages of sin is death," it means spiritual death, not physical death.

When we lose the empowerment of the Spirit, we lose soul-control to our sin nature. This can be momentary, it can be for an extended period, or if the believer never confesses sin, then the status of "carnality" (spiritual death) will go on indefinitely, accompanied by intensifying increments of Divine discipline for remaining out of the Power Zone—out of fellowship with God.

Diagram 4 should help us see why God invented the Power Zone for the earthly ministry of Christ: so He could execute the salvation phase of God's plan by enduring the greatest suffering in the history of humanity without committing a single act of sin. Jesus Christ then gave the Power Zone to us so we could live inside the same Power Zone that so effectively sustained Him.

> *Matt. 12:18; Luke 4:18 – Behold my Servant whom I have chosen; My Beloved in whom My soul is well pleased. I will put My Spirit upon Him. The Spirit of the Lord is upon Me.*

> *Eph. 1:19–20 – And what is the surpassing greatness of His power toward us who believe. These are according to the standard of His inner power, which has been operational in Christ.*

> *Eph. 6:10 – ... keep on becoming empowered by means of His conferred power.*

Acquiring Our Human Spirit and Understanding Its Purpose

In addition to our indwelling and empowerment by the Holy Spirit, there is yet another "spirit'" that is absolutely required to be operative before we can live the Spirit-Directed Life. This other spirit is the human spirit.

As we saw in diagrams 1 and 2, God gave us soul life along with our physical life at the moment of birth. However, we don't receive our human spirit until the moment of salvation. We have no need for a human spirit until we become spiritually alive, as shown in diagram 5.

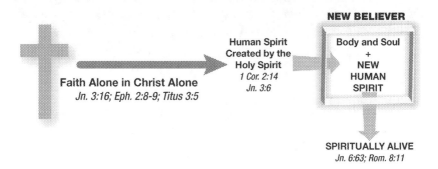

DIAGRAM 5: Acquisition of Our Human Spirit

At the moment of salvation, the only information inside our brand-new human spirit is the gospel of Christ. The author of the book of Hebrews (most likely Apollos) makes it very clear that we are to advance spiritually beyond the gospel of Christ and grow into spiritually mature believers:

> *Heb. 6:1 – Therefore leaving the elementary teaching about the Christ, let us press on to maturity, not laying again a foundation of repentance from dead works and of faith toward God, of instruction about baptisms, and laying on of hands, and the resurrection of the dead and eternal judgment.*

The purpose of the teaching ministry of the Holy Spirit is to teach the word of God to our human spirit so our spiritual house begins to acquire spiritual furniture. The spiritual furniture becomes our spiritual arsenal for spiritual warfare. However, in order to build up our spiritual arsenal, we have to be inside the Power Zone. Why? Because the Holy Spirit will obviously not be teaching our human spirit as long as the Spirit is grieved through sin, Eph. 4:30, or quenched through failure to confess sin, 1 Thes. 5:19.

If you will recall from diagram 1, at the moment of physical birth we did not have a human spirit. There was no need for us to have a human spirit as unbelievers, because the human spirit has function only in the life of the believer. Therefore, unbelievers who claim to have had a "spiritual experience" are speaking under the influence of their own soul gas. Outside of salvation or demon possession, unbelievers cannot have a spiritual experience because they are not Spirit indwelled or empowered and have no human spirit. Therefore, apart from accepting Christ as savior, or demonism, a spiritual experience is impossible for unbelievers.

As previously mentioned, the human spirit has three synergetic purposes in the Christian life, each working together to advance our spiritual growth, as diagram 6 shows.

DIAGRAM 6: Three Synergetic Purposes of Our Human Spirit

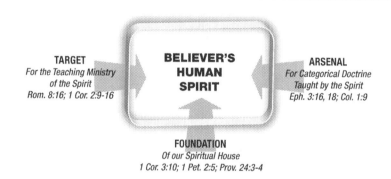

The three purposes for our human spirit are focused around our spiritual growth. The amount of doctrine (God's word) inside of our human spirit determines our spiritual I.Q. The higher our spiritual I.Q., the greater our application of doctrine to our circumstances. The greater our application, the greater our capacity for life, love, and happiness.

The Grace Bypass of Human I.Q.

For unbelievers, application of God's word to personal circumstances is impossible, because the word of God can be understood only through the teaching ministry of the Holy Spirit to the human spirit. The only reason an unbeliever can understand the gospel of Christ is because the Holy Spirit makes the salvation issue clear.

1 Cor. 2:14 – But the natural man does not accept the things of the Spirit of God; he cannot understand them because they are spiritually discerned.

For the unbeliever, the application system for dealing with life is limited by genetics and worldly influence, as shown in diagram 7.

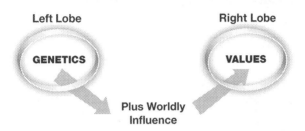

DIAGRAM 7: UNBELIEVERS APPLICATION SYSTEM

Left Lobe   Right Lobe

GENETICS   VALUES

Plus Worldly
Influence

For believers in Christ, God has found a way to bypass the inequalities of our genetically acquired human I.Q. and give us the opportunity to use the Power Zone as our application system. As long as we are inside the Power Zone where the teaching ministry of the Spirit takes place, our application system for dealing with life takes on a whole new perspective, as illustrated by diagram 8.

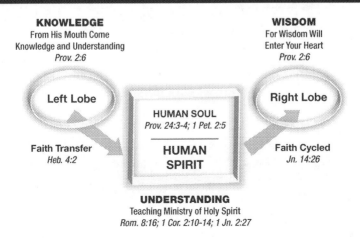

DIAGRAM 8: BELIEVERS APPLICATION SYSTEM THROUGH THE POWER ZONE

KNOWLEDGE
From His Mouth Come
Knowledge and Understanding
Prov. 2:6

WISDOM
For Wisdom Will
Enter Your Heart
Prov. 2:6

Left Lobe   Right Lobe

HUMAN SOUL
Prov. 24:3-4; 1 Pet. 2:5

HUMAN SPIRIT

Faith Transfer
Heb. 4:2

Faith Cycled
Jn. 14:26

UNDERSTANDING
Teaching Ministry of Holy Spirit
Rom. 8:16; 1 Cor. 2:10-14; 1 Jn. 2:27

As long as we are inside the Power Zone and believe the word of God, the teaching ministry of the Holy Spirit is operational. The Spirit bypasses our human I.Q. and teaches God's word to our human spirit. Heb. 4:2 makes it clear that the word of God must be believed—mixed with faith—for the Spirit's teaching ministry to function:

> *For indeed we have had good news preached to us, just as they also [Exodus generation of Jews]; But the word they heard did not profit them, because it was not mixed with faith in those who heard.*

Once the Spirit teaches our human spirit so that God's word is understood, we begin to fill up our spiritual house (human soul) with categories of scripture. As long as we remain inside the Power Zone, we cycle God's word as needed (Jn. 14:26) into the right lobe (heart) for application. All application of God's word to circumstances occurs from the right lobe, or the heart. That's why God is so interested in what is in our hearts:

> *1 Tim. 1:5; Jer. 17:10; Heb. 4:12 – But the goal of our instruction is love from a pure heart and a good conscience and a true faith ... I the Lord search the heart ... the word of God is ... a critic of thoughts and intentions of the heart.*

You can see in diagram 8 that the human spirit is the "foundation" of our spiritual house, which is the soul. It should be obvious at this point that the primary objective for all believers after salvation is to replace the human viewpoint in our right lobes with the Divine viewpoint—in other words, fill up our spiritual house with the spiritual furniture of God's word and cycle it into our right lobes for application to our circumstances. As we begin to do this, our capacity for love, life, happiness, and prosperity increases dramatically, along with our ability to deal with the inevitable pressures and adversities of daily living.

1 Pet. 2:5 says we are "being built up as a spiritual house." That is a specific reference to spiritual growth, which is only possible through the teaching ministry of the Holy Spirit to our human spirit. Why doesn't the Spirit teach only the left lobe of the brain? Because, through genetics, human I.Q. differs from person to person by such a wide margin that it can range anywhere from moron to genius levels. Because of this obvious inequality, the teaching ministry of the Spirit levels the playing field, bypasses human I.Q., and teaches only the human spirit.

> *Jn. 14:26 – But the Helper, the Holy Spirit, whom the Father will send in my name, He will teach you all things, and bring to your remembrance all that I said to you.*

> *Jn. 16:13–14 – But when He, the Spirit of truth comes, He will guide you into all the truth, for He will not speak on His own initiative, but whatever He hears, He will speak; and He will disclose to you ...*

> *1 Cor. 2:11–13 – ... the thoughts of God no one knows except the Spirit of God. Now we have received, not the spirit of the world, but the Spirit who is from God, that we might know the things freely given to us by God, which things we also speak, not in words taught by human wisdom, but in those taught by the Spirit, combining spiritual thoughts with spiritual words.*

> *Rom. 8:16 – The Spirit Himself bears witness with our spirit that we are the children of God.*

Because of the grace provision of the teaching ministry of the Holy Spirit, all believers have an equal opportunity to understand the word of God and to grow spiritually, regardless of their human I.Q. Is that grace or what? God's plan for you and me is not limited by human genetics. The only thing that ever limits our spiritual advancement is our own failure to live inside the Power Zone, which is the only place we can grow spiritually and have fellowship with God:

1 John 1:6–7 – If we say that we have fellowship with Him and yet walk in darkness [sin], we lie and do not practice the truth. But if we walk in the light [Power Zone] we have fellowship with one another and the blood of Jesus His Son cleanses us from all sin.

If there was ever any doubt that the cross is the only reason why confession of sin is effective for getting us back in fellowship with God in the Power Zone, verse 7 should erase that doubt. You will notice that verses 6 and 7 are not about salvation, they are about recovery from sin. In fact, 1 Jn. 1:7–9 makes it clear that the cross is what allows us to get back inside the Power Zone simply by confession of sin. It is not an accident that the Apostle John places verses 6–9 back to back so we will know that only the cross makes confession of sin effective in restoring us to fellowship with God after sin:

1 John 1:7 – ... the blood of Jesus His Son cleanses us from all sin.

1 John 1:8–9 – If we say that we have no sin, we are deceiving ourselves and the truth is not in us. If we confess our sins, He is faithful and righteous to forgive us our sins and to cleanse us from all unrighteousness.

If we want to have fellowship with God, we must first be cleansed of sin. If we want to live inside the Power Zone, where all the ministries of the Spirit are available, keeping short accounts with God through confession of sin is the only way it's going to happen.

The Ultimate Implant

As we have seen, unbelievers have a soul, but they are missing the Holy Spirit and a human spirit. Therefore, except for salvation or being possessed by demonic spirits, no spiritual experience is possible for the unbeliever. On the other hand, as believers we cannot be demon possessed, because our body is the temple of the Holy Spirit, and a demon cannot enter a Spirit- indwelled body and soul:

> *2 Cor. 6:16 – ... For we are the temple of the living God.*

This passage brings up an interesting point. As believers in Christ, in a sense we are all a "walking church." Think about it: In the Old Testament, the physical structure of the Jewish church, the temple itself, was holy, because it was indwelled by God—only the Jewish Levitical priests were allowed to enter the holy temple—but in the Church Age it is the believer in Christ that is now indwelled by God.

> *1 Cor. 3:16–17 – Do you not know that you are a temple of God, and that the Spirit of God dwells in you? ... for the temple of God is holy, and that is what you are.*

How does all this relate to the Power Zone? Immediately after the Father had judged Christ for our sins, Christ said, "It is finished," and at that moment the veil in the holy temple was split from top to bottom. What did that mean? It meant that Christ, by paying for our sins, had just made the Power Zone available to all believers. It meant that every believer would soon be a priest and therefore have direct access to God. It meant the end of the Levitical priesthood and the beginning of a universal priesthood—the priesthood of the believer. It meant that the universal indwelling and empowerment of the Spirit inside every believer would soon become available for the first time in human history. In other words, in the Church Age, the Power Zone became the new "holy place," and we live in that holy place when we are controlled by the Spirit. It is precisely the holy place, the Power Zone, that the Bible is referring to in passages such as "abide in Me," "walk in Him," "walk in the light," "walk in the Spirit," "be filled with the Spirit," and so forth.

Prior to the splitting of the veil, only the Levitical priests could enter the holy of holies in the temple. But today, every believer is in permanent union with Christ and therefore permanently indwelled by the Spirit. This opens up the option of also being empowered by the Spirit. Since every believer is now a priest, fellowship with God is available to every believer-priest who currently resides inside the Power Zone. Heb.10:19–20 makes this clear:

> *Since therefore, believers, we have confidence to enter the holy place [fellowship with God inside the Power Zone] by the blood of Jesus, by a new and living way which He inaugurated for us through the veil, that is, His flesh ...*

In the Church Age, the Power Zone is now the holy place—a new and living way. Since every believer is now a priest, we are the sanctuary, not the church auditorium. Therefore, there is no point in inviting the Spirit into the auditorium. He is in you! And since every believer is a believer-priest, functionally we have replaced the Levitical priests in representing ourselves before God, and the Mosaic Law has been replaced by a higher law, the law of spirituality:

> *Heb. 7:12 – For when the priesthood is changed, of necessity there takes place a change of law also.*

> *1 Pet.2:5, 9 – You also, as living stones, are being built up as a spiritual house for a holy priesthood ... a chosen race, a royal priesthood, a holy nation.*

God's grace provision of empowering every believer priest with the Holy Spirit could not be foreseen by Satan, because it was hidden in God until the Church Age, Eph. 3:3–12; Col. 1:26. The Power Zone is a major part of the mystery doctrine mentioned so frequently in the New Testament. The availability of the Power Zone caught Satan by surprise, and as a control freak, he doesn't like surprises. He will use every form of sin, human good, and evil to keep us out of the Power Zone and within the spiritual death zones. Satan is smart enough to see that, humanly speaking, we don't have the power to live the Christian life. But we don't have to have the power, all we need is the will; God has the power.

In Chapter 4, we will see how to access God's power by "Exploiting Grace in the Phone Zone."

CHAPTER 3 KEY POINTS

- God gave us the Holy Spirit at salvation for at least five reasons: Fellowship with Him; Empowerment; Spiritual growth; Production; Effective prayer. (p. 43)
- Personal sin causes spiritual death and separates us from God immediately. (p. 44)
- There are four categories of sin nature production: Sin; Human good; Self-gratification; Self-denial. (p. 47)
- The Security Zone represents our position in Christ, but the Power Zone is the only place where the Spirit can direct our lives. (p. 50)
- If we are inside the Power Zone, we are spiritually alive. If we are outside the Power Zone, we are spiritually dead. (p. 51)
- Personal sin causes the transfer of soul-control from the Spirit to our sin nature. (p. 51)
- The amount of doctrine (God's word) inside our human spirit determines our spiritual I.Q. (p. 54)
- The Holy Spirit bypasses our human I.Q. and teaches God's word to our human spirit. (p. 56)
- Humanly speaking, we don't have the power to live the Christian life, but we don't have to have the power, all we need is the will; God has the power. (p. 60-61)

CHAPTER 4: EXPLOITING GRACE IN THE PHONE ZONE

The "Phone-Home" Prayer

This chapter is about the Phone Zone for an obvious reason. Personal sin interrupts our fellowship with God. It is our responsibility to phone home to restore fellowship with God, because we made a conscious choice to sin. Sin causes us to be living inside one of the spiritual death zones from which we can still recover by using the grace provision of the Phone Zone.

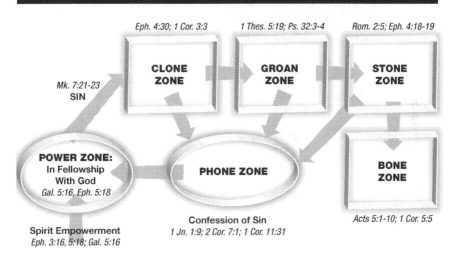

DIAGRAM 1: Spiritual Death Zones Powered by Our Sin Nature

Eph. 4:30; 1 Cor. 3:3   1 Thes. 5:19; Ps. 32:3-4   Rom. 2:5; Eph. 4:18-19

CLONE ZONE   **GROAN ZONE**   **STONE ZONE**

Mk. 7:21-23 **SIN**

POWER ZONE: In Fellowship With God Gal. 5:16, Eph. 5:18

PHONE ZONE

BONE ZONE

Spirit Empowerment Eph. 3:16, 5:18; Gal. 5:16

Confession of Sin 1 Jn. 1:9; 2 Cor. 7:1; 1 Cor. 11:31

Acts 5:1-10; 1 Cor. 5:5

Sin causes us to become AWOGL (absent without God's leave) from the Power Zone. This means we are now under the power of our sin nature instead of the power of the Spirit. If and when we are willing to use it, God provides a special phone-home prayer that allows us to recover fellowship with Him instantly. The phone-home prayer is combined in the same verse with a promise to cleanse us from sin and restore us completely to fellowship with God. To recover this fellowship after sin, we simply phone home through the grace provision of 1 John 1:9:

> *If we confess our sins, He is faithful and righteous to forgive us our sins and to cleanse us from all unrighteousness.*

The Greek word for "confess" is *homologeo*, which is a legal term meaning to cite your own guilt. By confessing our sins directly to God the Father, we are citing a previous case in which a judgment was made. The judgment specifically refers to the cross, where the Father judged the Son for our sins. Whether we realize it or not, when we confess sin, we are citing that judgment. The reason we are forgiven within a fraction of a second of our confession is that the Father must honor the work of the Son. Since Christ did all the work, there is not one ounce of human merit in confession of sin.

In Christianity today, there are a few critics of God's grace policy of confession for restoration to fellowship. The critics say that confession of sin is human works or contend that it isn't necessary. Calling confession of sin "human works" is actually one of the worst forms of blasphemy. Why? Because, through confession or any other means, we have actually done nothing to earn the privilege of fellowship with God.

God remains so impressed with the work of His Son on the cross that He has made recovery of fellowship with Him after sin totally dependent upon His Son's work. The fact that Christ paid for our sins on the cross is the only reason that we can be forgiven. Christ died both for the sins we commit before and after our salvation. Confession of sin is a daily reminder that the cross remains the most significant event in all of human history. The cross is the greatest strategic victory for grace in the history of the universe. The only reason for the grace provision of restoration to fellowship simply by confession of sin is because the Father's grace policy is based on His Son's work, not ours. Confession is not "human works." Nor is confession a license to sin; it is a renewal of our empowerment to serve, and that is why it is necessary.

Unclean and Unaware

Partly because of the critics of God's grace policies, and partly because of the failure to rightly divide the word of truth, many Christians are unaware that confession of sin is required to recover fellowship with God after sin. Furthermore, when confession of sin is actually taught, it is almost never taught as the only means to recover fellowship with God and to ensure that all ministries of the Holy Spirit to the individual believer are operational.

As previously listed, there are at least five things that totally depend upon confession of sin:

- Recovering fellowship with God
- Empowerment by the Spirit
- Spiritual growth
- Production
- Effective prayer

All these things require the empowerment of the Spirit inside the Power Zone. How many times have we been taught about the "fruits of the Spirit" without ever hearing anything about confession of sin so we can be empowered to produce them? How many times have we been taught about prayer without being reminded of the importance of getting back in fellowship through confession before we pray? It is impossible to have fellowship with God, grow and produce spiritually, and pray effectively unless we are empowered by the Spirit. We cannot be empowered by the Spirit without confession of sin.

The implications of the ignorance of this basic Biblical principle almost defy words. However, two words pretty much sum up the implications: unclean and unaware. We are unclean to God every time we defile ourselves by sin. Many Christians today are unaware of the consequent loss of empowerment by the Spirit caused by sin. The problem of being unclean and unaware is solved with the grace provision of confession of sin.

One purpose of this book is to connect the dots between the "how" of getting back into fellowship with God after sin and the result of being in fellowship, which is production acceptable to God through the power of the Spirit.

> *Eph. 4:30; 1 Thes. 5:19 – Do not grieve ... do not quench the Holy Spirit ...*
>
> *Eph. 5:18 – ... but be filled with [empowered by] the Spirit ...*
>
> *Rom. 12:2 – ... that you may prove what the will of God is, that which is good and acceptable and perfect.*
>
> *Gal. 5:22–23 – ... the fruit of the Spirit is love, joy, peace, patience, kindness, goodness, faithfulness, gentleness, self-control ...*

Through the grace provision of 1 Jn. 1:9, God has provided a way to allow sinful believers to get back into fellowship with Him after sin. Without this grace provision, we could never operate under the power of the Holy Spirit, and we could never live the Spirit-Directed Life. Therefore, after the grace gifts of salvation and the Power Zone, the next greatest grace provision for living the Christian life is confession of sin. We can't get back inside the Power Zone without using the grace provision of the Phone Zone.

The grace provision of confession is a mental activity, not an overt act, and our restoration to fellowship and empowerment depends entirely on our willingness to do it. Most Christians would be more than willing to do whatever is required, so willingness is not the problem. The problem is that many believers are not being made aware that fellowship with God and empowerment of the Spirit is lost through sin and that recovery can be achieved only through naming our sins to God. Sin gets us out of the Power Zone, and confession of sin gets us back into it. Confession is the only cleansing mechanism that gets us back in the Power Zone, where the Spirit can direct our lives. How do we know this?

Before this question is answered, let's review what sin does to us, according to the words of Jesus Christ:

> *Mark 7:14b–15, 20–23 – "Listen to Me, all of you, and understand: there is nothing outside the man which going into him can defile him; but the things which proceed out of the man are what defile the man. For from within, out of the heart of men, proceed the evil thoughts and fornications, thefts, murders, adulteries, deeds of coveting and wickedness, as well as deceit, sensuality, envy, slander, pride and foolishness. All these evil things proceed from within and defile the man"*

The word for "defile" in the Greek is *koinoo* (coino-oh), which means "to render unholy or unclean." Sin makes us unclean to God. When we are unclean to God, we are spiritually dead. Why? Because in addition to defiling ourselves before God, we have "grieved" and possibly "quenched" the Holy Spirit, according to Eph. 4:30; 1 Thes. 5:19. When we grieve the Spirit, we have put ourselves in the Clone Zone. When we quench the Spirit, we have degenerated into the Groan Zone. If we continue to fail to name sins to God, we will eventually degenerate into the Stone Zone, where we risk being placed into the Bone Zone by the wrath of God. Regardless of which spiritual death zone we are in, the source of sin is our ever-present sin nature, with its lust patterns:

> *James 1:14–15 – But each one is tempted when he is carried away and enticed by his own lust. Then when lust has conceived [we say yes to temptation], it gives birth to sin; and when sin is accomplished, it brings forth death [spiritual death].*

When we become spiritually dead due to personal sin, God can no longer have fellowship with us until we are cleansed.

Only a grace provision from God can cleanse us, and God has made it abundantly clear what that grace provision is. Besides the phone-home provision of 1 John 1:9, there are numerous other phone-home passages telling us to make confession of sins our top priority when we are out of fellowship.

> *1 Cor. 11:31 – ... if we judge ourselves, we will not be judged.*
>
> *2 Cor. 7:1 – Therefore, having these promises, believers, let us cleanse ourselves from all defilement of flesh and spirit, perfecting holiness in the fear of God.*
>
> *Rom. 6:12–13 – Therefore do not let sin reign in your mortal body that you should obey its lusts, and do not go on presenting the members of your body to sin as instruments of unrighteousness; but present yourselves to God as those alive from the dead.*
>
> *2 Tim. 2:21 – ... if a man cleanses himself from these things, he will be a vessel for honor, sanctified, useful to the Master, prepared for every good work.*
>
> *Rom. 6:19 – ... present your members as slaves to righteousness, resulting in sanctification.*
>
> *Rom. 12:1 – ... present your bodies as living sacrifice, holy, acceptable to God, which is your spiritual service of worship.*
>
> *Eph. 4:22–23 – ... lay aside the old self ... and ... be renewed in the spirit of your mind.*
>
> *Eph. 5:14 – ... awake sleeper, and arise from the dead, and Christ will shine on you.*

*Heb. 12:1 – ... let us also lay aside every encumbrance,
and the sin which so easily entangles us, and let us
run with endurance the race that is set before us.*

*Heb. 12:12–13 – ... strengthen the hands that are
weak and the knees that are feeble, and make straight
paths for your feet.*

*1 Jn. 3:3 – And everyone who has this hope fixed on
Him purifies himself, just as He is pure.*

*Rev. 3:19–20 – Those whom I love [believers], I
reprove and discipline; be diligent therefore, and
repent [return to the Power Zone]. Behold, I stand at
the door and knock [warning discipline]; if anyone
hears My voice and opens the door [confesses sin],
I will come in to him, and will dine with him [have
fellowship], and he with Me.*

*Jm. 1:8 and 4:8 – A double-minded man is unstable
in all his ways. Draw near to God and He will draw
near to you. Cleanse your hands, you sinners; and
purify your hearts, you double-minded.*

James 1:8 and 4:8 tell us to stop being a dork, a dipstick, through failure to confess sins. The word for "double-minded" is *dipsuchos*, which means to have a "double soul." A *dipsuchos* believer is a dipstick. Dipsticks are Christians who seldom confess sins and therefore rarely have the power to live the Spirit-Directed Life. They will dip their soul into everything that is not God's will for their life, from false doctrine to raunchy relationships. If raunchy relationships are the problem, they will sow their wild oats and then pray for a crop failure! They spend their time in a frantic search for happiness outside of God's will by dipping into various types of sin, then expecting God to nullify the effects of sin and their failure to confess it. They lack capacity for love because their lifestyle has placed scar tissue on their soul. They may attend church, but they attend as double-minded dipsticks, usually controlled by their sin nature. They can stop being dipsticks by doing two things: confessing sin and growing spiritually. However, spiritual growth takes time, and dipsticks have other priorities. To be fair, though, let's not forget that at one time or another we have all been dipsticks.

Confession of Sin: A Prayer and a Promise

Confession of sin is simultaneously a prayer and a promise. It is a prayer because we go before the throne of grace in personal petition. It is a promise because God promises to place us back inside the Power Zone every single time we name our sins to Him. There are no exceptions. Confession of sin refers back to the cross, because that's where Christ took our place in paying the penalty of His own spiritual death for our sins. Once we confess our sins, our Divine discipline may continue, but we will be inside the Power Zone and therefore able to handle it. Divine discipline becomes unbearable outside the Power Zone because we have lost the power of the Spirit to deal with it.

Essentially, confession of sin is coming clean with God about sin because we desire to be back in fellowship with Him ... back in the Power Zone. We do not need to specifically ask God to place us back in the Power Zone during confession because 1 John 1:9 and companion verses promise us restoration to fellowship. It is impossible for God not to honor His promises, because as believers we are permanently in union with Christ in the Security Zone. Diagram 2 will serve as a reminder about the Security and Power Zones:

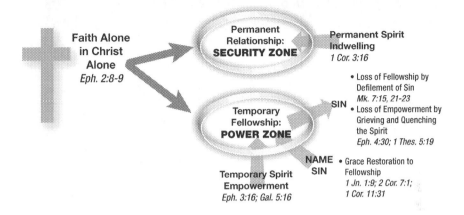

DIAGRAM 2: Reminder – Security and Power Zones

Faith Alone in Christ Alone
Eph. 2:8-9

Permanent Relationship: **SECURITY ZONE**

Permanent Spirit Indwelling
1 Cor. 3:16

SIN

Temporary Fellowship: **POWER ZONE**

• Loss of Fellowship by Defilement of Sin
  Mk. 7:15, 21-23
• Loss of Empowerment by Grieving and Quenching the Spirit
  Eph. 4:30; 1 Thes. 5:19

NAME
SIN

Temporary Spirit Empowerment
Eph. 3:16; Gal. 5:16

• Grace Restoration to Fellowship
  1 Jn. 1:9; 2 Cor. 7:1; 1 Cor. 11:31

Is confession necessary to restore fellowship and empowerment? If you have checked out the scripture references provided, you should be convinced that the answer to this question is one huge, honking YES! But just in case you aren't convinced or you need a reminder, let's look at who in the Bible says that confession of sin is necessary.

Jesus Christ: First to Teach the Disciples about Confession of Sin

Since forgiveness of sin is only possible through Christ's work on the cross, guess who first taught the disciples about the importance of confession of sin? It was Jesus Himself! In John 13:6–10, He teaches the disciples about confession of sin by washing their feet. He tells them in verse 7 that they will not understand what He is teaching them until later. Why later? Because they had to wait until the teaching ministry of the Spirit made it clear, and that won't happen until the Day of Pentecost. Unfortunately, many churches today don't understand that John 13:6–10 is about confession of sin. Let's take a close look at that passage.

Jesus and the Disciples have just finished the Last Supper; Jesus removes his outer garments, drapes a towel around his neck, grabs a basin of water, and begins to wash the Disciples' feet. Jesus is well aware that He has only a few more hours to live, so anything He does or says to the Disciples is of major importance. He is about to teach them one of the most essential and most neglected doctrines of the Church Age, the importance of daily confession of sin.

The disciples are conscious that Christ is playing the role of a servant in this scenario, and they are very uncomfortable with that, realizing that the roles should be reversed. In verse 6, Peter says, basically, "Lord, you're not going to wash my feet, are you?" In the next verse, Jesus replies, "You won't understand what I'm doing until later," and that statement should tip us off that a lot more than just foot-washing is going on here. A child could have walked into that room and understood that Jesus was in the role of a foot-washing servant, and yet, Jesus tells adult disciples that they will not understand what he is doing.

Not only is Jesus not teaching "service" here, but what He is teaching should always occur prior to service. Otherwise, the service being performed might be human good instead of Divine good. I will deal with these two important issues later.

In verse 8, Peter answers Jesus, saying, "You're not ever going to wash my feet," to which Jesus replies, "If I don't wash your feet, you can have nothing to do with Me." And what does that mean? It means that Peter can't have fellowship with Him because he is still unclean.

In verse 9, Peter responds, "Well, in that case, don't just wash my feet, wash my hands and my head too." Jesus says to Peter in verse 10, "He who is washed [already saved] needs only to wash his feet [confession of sins], and then will be totally clean [back inside the Power Zone, in fellowship with God, and empowered by the Spirit]." To help clear this up, the original Greek words for "washed" and "wash" are helpful:

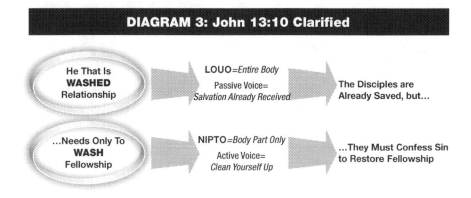

DIAGRAM 3: John 13:10 Clarified

| He That Is **WASHED** Relationship | → | LOUO=*Entire Body* Passive Voice= *Salvation Already Received* | → | The Disciples are Already Saved, but... |
| ...Needs Only To **WASH** Fellowship | → | NIPTO=*Body Part Only* Active Voice= *Clean Yourself Up* | → | ...They Must Confess Sin to Restore Fellowship |

In verse 12, when Jesus had completed the foot-washing, He asked if they knew what He had done to them. They obviously did not. Jesus had just taught them God cannot have fellowship with a defiled (sinful) believer, and that confession restores the believer 100 percent to fellowship. The disciples would not understand this until the teaching ministry of the Spirit was made available to them as Apostles inside the Power Zone.

Besides Jesus Himself, who else says confession of sin is necessary? The Apostle John obviously realized what Jesus was teaching him and the other disciples in John 13, as John wrote 1 John 1:9. Likewise, the writer of Hebrews encourages us to get back in fellowship after sin. James encourages us not to become double-minded by failure to confess sin. The Apostle Paul steps up to the plate on numerous occasions concerning confession, as evidenced by the passages just listed in Romans, Corinthians, Ephesians, and 2 Timothy. It is also Paul who tells us that we need to frequently check our soul status to see if we are in or out of fellowship:

> *2 Cor. 13:5 – Test yourselves to see if you are in the faith; examine yourselves!*

How do we go about doing that? What is the first clue that we are out of fellowship? Here are some basic rules of thumb we can apply:

- Do we have inner peace, or do we have worry, fear, and anxiety?
- Do we direct impersonal love toward others, or mental-attitude-sins?
- Are we trying to get along without compromising doctrine, or are we being implacable and vindictive?
- Are we able to forgive and forget, or are we leashed up to unforgiveness?
- Are we looking forward to what God has for us, or are we depressed and in slavery to the past?
- Is our thought pattern positive or negative?
- Do we have an attitude of gratitude or bitterness?
- What is our attitude toward confession of sin? Do we think we are such a special believer that confession just doesn't apply to us?
- Are we aware that the only person to whom confession never applied is Jesus Christ?

The need for coming clean with God through confession of sin has never changed. David makes that clear in the Old Testament:

> *Pss. 32:3–5 – When I kept silent about my sin, my body wasted away through all my groaning all day long. For day and night Your hand was heavy upon me; My vitality was drained away as with the fever-heat of summer. I named my sin to You, and my iniquity I did not hide; I said "I will confess my transgressions to the Lord"; and You forgave the guilt of my sin.*

The purpose of confession of sin is so God can cleanse us and restore us to fellowship and empowerment. The reason confession is effective is that Christ paid the penalty for our sins on the Cross. God made it clear to Old Testament believers, just as He has made it clear to us, that we must be presentable to Him before He can have fellowship with us. In the presence of God at the burning bush, Moses was told by God:

> *Ex. 3:5 – ..."do not come near here; remove your sandals from your feet, for the place on which you are standing is holy ground."*

Before the Levitical priests could enter the temple, they had to wash their hands in a symbolic gesture of being cleansed from sin. Today, we are warned as Church Age believers not to partake of the communion elements if we are out of fellowship with God:

> *1 Cor. 11:27–30 – Therefore whoever eats the bread or drinks the cup of the Lord in an unworthy manner [out of fellowship with God], shall be guilty of the body and blood of the Lord [blasphemy]. But let a man examine himself, and so let him eat of the bread and drink of the cup. For he who eats and drinks, eats and drinks judgment to himself, if he does not judge the body rightly [in fellowship through confession of sin]. For this reason many among you are weak and sick, and a number sleep.*

If you attend a church that does not remind you to examine yourself prior to communion, let this chapter serve as a reminder of the importance of doing so.

How Do We Know that Confession of Sin Restores Us to Fellowship with God?

The answer to this question is simple—because the word of God tells us it does. In the first section of this chapter, I listed back-to-back verses that tell us to make confession of sin our top priority when we are out of fellowship. Those verses are either the *principle* behind 1 Jn. 1:9 or the *mechanics* of 1 Jn. 1:9. As a reminder of what those verses told us, here's what happens when we confess our sins:

1 Cor. 11:31 – ... we will not be judged
2 Cor. 7:1 – ... we are perfecting holiness
Rom. 6:13 – ... we are alive from the dead
2 Tim. 2:21 – ... we are a vessel of honor, sanctified, useful to the Master, prepared for every good work
Rom. 6:19 – ... slaves to righteousness, resulting in sanctification
Rom. 12:1 – ... acceptable to God, which is your spiritual service of worship
Eph. 4:22 – ... we have laid aside the old self [sin nature]
Eph. 5:14 – ... we have arisen from the dead, and Christ will shine on you
Heb. 12:1 – ... we can now run with endurance
Heb. 12:13 – ... the Spirit can now make straight paths for our feet
1 Jn. 3:3 – ... purifies himself [confession restores fellowship]
Rev. 3:20 – ... I [Christ] will come in to him, and will dine with him [fellowship]
Jm. 4:8 – ... God ... will draw near to you [fellowship]

Confession of sin is the only way to approach God the Father after we have sinned, because there is no other way to restore fellowship with Him that conforms to God's policy of grace. Recovery from sin must be compatible with at least five grace criteria:

1. Confession Excludes Human Merit: Since forgiveness of sin depends on the effectiveness of Christ's work, confession of sin is without human merit.

    Jn. 15:5 – Apart from Me, you can do nothing.

2. Confession is Effective Immediately: No time delay is mentioned in 1 Jn.1:9. If we confess our sins, God is faithful and righteous to forgive us and to cleanse us from

all unrighteousness.

3. Confession is Absolute: Confession of sin provides 100 percent restoration to fellowship.

   2 Cor. 7:1 – ... let us cleanse ourselves of all defilement of flesh and spirit, perfecting holiness ...

   Rom. 8:5–6 – For those who are according to the flesh set their minds on the things of the flesh, but those who are according to the Spirit, the things of the Spirit.

   Titus 1:15 – To the pure, all things are pure ...

4. Confession is Simple: If we name our known sins, God forgives our unknown sins as well.

   1 Jn. 1:9 – ... He is faithful and righteous to forgive us our sins [known] and to cleanse us from all unrighteousness [unknown sins].

5. Confession is Liberating: Confession frees God to forgive us so that we may serve Him. Since God forgets our sins after we confess them, that's exactly what He wants us to do about our sins. We are to avoid worthless systems of ritual, penance, and additional sins like a guilt complex.

   Ps. 103:12 – As far as the East is from the West, so far has He removed our sins from us.

   Isa. 43:25 – ... I will not remember your sins.

   Phil. 3:13 – ... forgetting what lies behind and reaching forward to what lies ahead.

Our Freedom of Choice Determines Soul-Control

It is obvious that God created both angels and man with freedom of choice. As free agents, we might obey God's word and confess our sins, and we might not. Satan used his freewill to revolt against God in Isaiah 14:13–14, and obviously Adam and Eve used their freewill to revolt against God in the Garden. Even after salvation, we still retain our sin nature and our freedom of choice. The inevitable result of that combination is that we will continue to sin. Angelic and human freewill decisions, both for good and bad, are evident from Genesis to Revelation.

Once we use our freedom of choice to accept Christ as Savior, there is no doubt that eternal life in the Security Zone is permanently ours. Why should we be so concerned about our freewill decisions in the Power Zone once we have eternal life in the Security Zone? The answer is, because the Christian life can only be lived inside the Power Zone. Unconfessed sins keep us separated from God through defilement, while grieving and quenching the Spirit. If sins remain unconfessed, we harden our heart and open the door to the sin unto death. The sin unto death is not a single sin but, rather, a lifestyle of sin in which debauchery and perversion become the norm and resultant scar tissue on the soul eventually prevents any possibility of recovery.

Our freewill decisions determine which of two competing powers controls our soul. Our freewill decisions determine if we will confess our daily sins to God and be empowered by the Spirit, or fail to do so and be empowered by our sin nature. The latter means living in the degenerative stages of spiritual death. It is our freewill decisions that keep us in fellowship with God or out of fellowship with God … that determine if we are spiritual or carnal … that determine if we are producing Divine good inside the Power Zone, or human good, sin, and evil in one of the spiritual death zones. Freewill decisions determine if we are accumulating or losing blessings in time and rewards in eternity. Freewill decisions determine if we are winners or losers in the spiritual warfare constantly raging over the issue of soul-control.

The Two Absolute States of Believer Soul-Control

In 1 Cor. 3:1 the Apostle Paul tells the Corinthian believers that they are not living in the Power Zone, but in one or more of the spiritual death zones (to review spiritual death zones, see diagram 1):

> *1 Cor. 3:1 – And I, believers, could not speak to you as to spiritual men, but as to carnal, as to babes in Christ.*

Paul is saying that they are like spiritual babies because they have been living outside the Power Zone. Instead of being under the Spirit's control, they have been controlled by their sin nature. This is just another of many passages that establishes that at any given moment after salvation, we are either spiritual or we are carnal.

It is important to understand that if we are only in the Clone Zone, the first stage of carnality, we are still 100 percent out of fellowship with God and 100 percent carnal. Carnality and spirituality are both absolute states of soul; we are either 100 percent spiritual, or we are 100 percent carnal. In other words, at any given moment after salvation, our soul is either 100 percent controlled by the Spirit, or 100 percent controlled by our sin nature. Let's document this Biblical truth right now, as the Bible is very clear about it.

In the following comparison, terms such as "no part," "flesh," and "defiled" refer to being controlled by our sin nature, while the terms "wash," "light," "pure," "obedience," and "Spirit" refer to being controlled by the Spirit. Contrast the scriptures below by reading first the verse in the "Sin Nature Control" column, then the verse in the "Spirit Control ("Power Zone")" column directly across from it. The comparison begins with Jesus Christ teaching the disciples about the importance of confession of sin in John 13:

SIN NATURE CONTROL	SPIRIT CONTROL (POWER ZONE)
Jn. 13: 8 – if I don't wash you [cleanse from sin] *you have no part with Me* [100 percent out of fellowship]	*Jn. 13: 10 – needs only to wash his feet* [name your sins] *but is completely clean* [100 percent back in fellowship]
Rom. 7: 18 – For I know that nothing good dwells in me, that is, in my flesh [sin nature]	*Eph. 5: 8-9 – walk as children of light* [Spirit control], *for the fruit of light consists of all goodness and righteousness and truth.*
Titus 1: 15b – but to those who are defiled [by sin] *nothing is pure.*	*Titus 1: 15a – To the pure* [in fellowship through confession] *all things are pure.*
Rom. 6: 16c – do you not know that ... you are slaves of the one whom you obey, either of sin resulting in death [spiritual death] ...	*Rom. 6: 16d – or of obedience resulting in righteousness?* [obedience of confession and restoration to fellowship]
Rom. 7:25b – but on the other hand, with my flesh the law of sin [out of fellowship, serving sin]	*Rom. 7: 25a – on the other hand, I myself with my mind am serving the law of God* [in fellowship under the new law of Spirituality]
Rom. 8:4c – do not walk according to the flesh [out of fellowship]	*Rom. 8: 4d – but according to the Spirit* [in fellowship]
Rom. 8:5a – For those who are according to the flesh, set their minds on the things of the flesh [sin control]	*Rom. 8:5b – but those who are according to the Spirit, on the things of the Spirit* [Spirit control]
Rom. 8:6a – the mind set on the flesh is death [spiritually dead, controlled by our sin nature]	*Rom. 8:6b – but the mind set on the Spirit is life and peace* [spiritually alive, Spirit control]
Rom. 8: 8 – and those who are in the flesh cannot please God [sin nature control]	*Gal. 5: 16 – walk by the Spirit and you will not carry out the desire of the flesh* [Spirit control]
Rom. 8 13a – for if you are living according to the flesh, you must die [spiritual death]	*Rom. 8: 13b – but if by the Spirit you are putting to death the deeds of the body, you will live* [spiritually alive, Spirit control]

It should be obvious from these contrasted verses that at any given moment we are either spiritual or we are carnal. It should also be obvious that we get out of the Power Zone through our freewill decisions to sin. The longer we remain out of the Power Zone, the more we intensify Divine discipline due to sinfulness while decreasing the likelihood of our recovery. Each stage in the spiritual death zones diagram indicates greater spiritual degeneration. In the process of this degeneration, our human spirit begins to atrophy due to our deliberate neglect of the word of God and our failure to return to fellowship with God through confession of sin.

Spiritual degeneration can be very subtle, because it occurs slowly, over a period of months and sometimes even years. It's so easy to gradually fail the prosperity test by forgetting the source of prosperity when things are going well. Forgetting that God is the source of our prosperity leads to apathy toward God's word. Spiritual degeneration frequently starts with apathy. When we become apathetic toward God's word, we consider ourselves smarter than God, we ignore basic doctrines, and we gradually become fools.

> *Rev. 3:16 – So because you are lukewarm, and neither hot nor cold, I will spit you out of My mouth.*

> *Rom. 1:21–22 – For even though they knew God, they did not honor Him as God, or give thanks; but they became futile in their speculations, and their foolish heart was darkened. Professing to be wise, they became fools.*

When our heart becomes darkened, it is because we have consistently failed in spiritual warfare over a long period of time. Since the issue in spiritual warfare is soul-control, let's take a closer look at the issue of who's in charge.

Spiritual Warfare and Soul-Control

As you can tell by the contrasting scriptures in the previous comparison, we are in constant spiritual warfare over the issue of soul-control. Gal. 5:16–17 makes this battle very clear:

> *But I say, walk by the Spirit, and you will not carry out the desire of the flesh [sin nature]. For the flesh sets its desire against the Spirit, and the Spirit against the flesh; for these are in opposition to one another, so that you may not do the things that you please.*

There are three characteristics of soul-control. It is

- choice driven
- mutually exclusive
- absolute

DIAGRAM 4: THREE CHARACTERISTICS OF SOUL-CONTROL IN SPIRITUAL WARFARE

The Holy Spirit and the sin nature are mutually exclusive because they have nothing in common and they are in constant battle for soul-control. The battle is choice driven because we choose the controller.

The result of the battle is absolute because only one controls at any given moment.

Keep in mind that we inherited our sin nature through physical birth, but we acquired the Holy Spirit through faith alone in Christ alone. Were it not for the power of the Spirit inside the Power Zone, we would have no possibility of spiritual victory over our sin nature. For Church Age believers, the gift of the Holy Spirit and the Power Zone is God's "trump" over the sin card that Satan played in the Garden. The point is that no matter what Satan does to attack us, God always has the solution.

Confession before Prayer: "Fess Up and Power Up"

The only reason we can approach God with confidence in prayer is because Christ solved the sin problem.

> *Heb. 4:16 – Let us therefore come boldly before the throne of grace that we may receive mercy and may find grace to help in time of need.*

> *Eph. 3:12 – ... in accordance with the eternal purpose which He carried out in Christ Jesus our Lord, in whom we have boldness and confident access through faith in Him.*

Naming our sins to God is the only prayer that God hears when we are spiritually dead due to sin. The reason for that is because sin defiles us before God, and He cannot have fellowship with sinful believers. Therefore, before God will hear us again, we have to take the grace option of naming our sins directly to him. If you are concerned about the accuracy of that statement, then consider the scripture references in diagram 5.

DIAGRAM 5: Why Confess Sin Prior to Prayer?

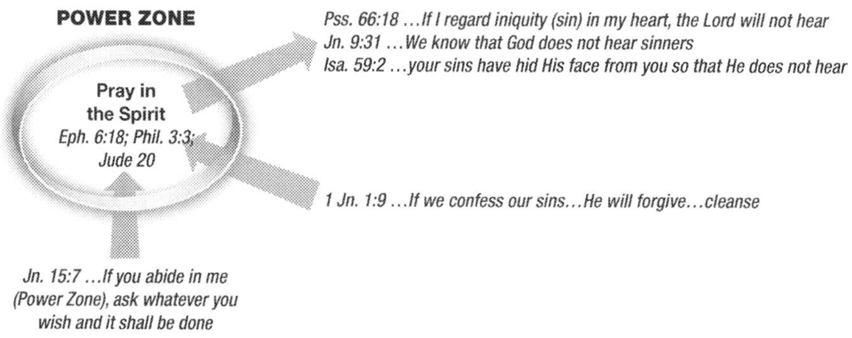

POWER ZONE

Pray in
the Spirit
Eph. 6:18; Phil. 3:3;
Jude 20

Pss. 66:18 ...If I regard iniquity (sin) in my heart, the Lord will not hear
Jn. 9:31 ...We know that God does not hear sinners
Isa. 59:2 ...your sins have hid His face from you so that He does not hear

1 Jn. 1:9 ...If we confess our sins...He will forgive...cleanse

Jn. 15:7 ...If you abide in me
(Power Zone), ask whatever you
wish and it shall be done

Prayer is one of the most powerful weapons in the believer's spiritual-warfare arsenal. But praying when we're out of fellowship with God because of unconfessed sin is like trying to drive a car that's out of gas. The car has great potential, but no power. The believer out of fellowship has potential, but no power. So fess up and power up!

If you are still in doubt that God hears the confession of sin prayer only when we are out of fellowship, then think back to the cross. During the final three hours on the cross, when Christ was bearing our sins, neither God the Father nor God the Holy Spirit could have anything to do with Christ, because He was being made "sin" for us.

> *Mark 15:34 – ... My God, My God, why have You forsaken Me?*

> *2 Cor. 5:21 – He made Him who knew no sin to become sin on our behalf, that we might become the righteousness of God in Him.*

Christ knew the answer to the question "Why have You forsaken Me?" but He wanted His question in writing in the Bible as additional evidence that God cannot have fellowship with us when we are defiled by sin. And so the question is this: if the Father and the Spirit could have nothing to do with the Son while He was being made sin for us, then what makes us think that They can have fellowship with us as sinful believers?

If you have been having a hard time living the Christian life recently, ask yourself if you have been living under the power of the Spirit or under the power of your sin nature. Have you been living in the Power Zone or in one of the spiritual death zones? If you are having a hard time getting your prayers answered, could it possibly be that you have been out of fellowship with God when you pray? By now, you should know exactly what to do about that.

This would also be a good place to point out that after naming our sins, we are going to be in a lot better position with our defense attorney in heaven, Jesus Christ, who will defend us against our accuser, the devil.

> *1 John 2:1 – My little children, I am writing these things to you that you may not sin. And if anyone sins, we have a defense attorney with the Father, Jesus Christ the righteous.*

> *Rev. 12:10 – ... for the accuser of believers has been thrown down, who accuses them before our God day and night.*

Diagrams 3 and 5 should make it very clear that the only prayer God hears when we are unclean due to sin is the confession-of-sin prayer, 1 John 1:9. If there is an exception, it would be when we are under such soul stress that we can't pray coherently for ourselves, in which case both the Son and Spirit pray for us, Rom. 8:26 and Heb. 7:25. Sometimes during great stress or trauma we are doing well just to utter, "God, help!" However, the point is to remain in fellowship during stressful times by applying God's word to our circumstances. Naming our sins returns soul-control to the Spirit so He can bring to our remembrance the appropriate doctrine at the right time:

Jn. 14:26 – ... the Holy Spirit ... will teach you all things, and bring to your remembrance all that I said to you.

We saw at the beginning of chapter 2 that our sins grieve and quench the Holy Spirit, thus separating us from God. And we saw in diagram 4 at the end of chapter 1 that there are explanatory phrases that tell us what happens to our relationship with God when we sin. Sin gets us out of fellowship with God—that is, out of the Power Zone. Sin places us in the Clone Zone, where Divine discipline begins. Continued failure to confess sins places us in the Groan Zone, where Divine discipline intensifies. Continued failure to confess sins places us in the Stone Zone, where Divine discipline is magnified and where the sin unto death may await us, in the Bone Zone. We will take this up in more detail in the chapters on the spiritual death zones. In the meantime, diagram 6 should serve as a reminder.

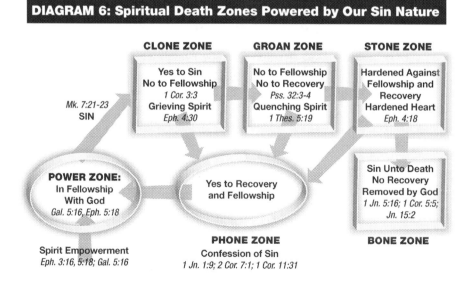

DIAGRAM 6: Spiritual Death Zones Powered by Our Sin Nature

Some believers may consider the concepts behind the Power Zone to be advanced doctrine, but I am here to tell you that the Power Zone is basic doctrine. Frankly, soul-control by the Holy Spirit is as basic as it gets, because we can't live the Christian life apart from the

Spirit's power. At the church that taught me practically everything I know, the concept of the Power Zone was one of the first things taught in basic Bible training. In the modern church, are we trying to be so creative and entertaining that we are failing to teach the basics? When it comes to teaching the word of God, my concept of creativity is, if it communicates, use it, but never sacrifice content for creativity. Let's first be creative in teaching the basics such as salvation and spirituality by grace.

This book, *The Power Zone*, is simply a creative documentation of the Spirit-Directed Life that God makes possible through His grace. One of God's grace provisions for living the Spirit-Directed Life is the Spirit's empowerment of spiritual gifts. Unfortunately, there is still some confusion about which spiritual gifts are operative in the Church Age and which ones are not. We will examine the issue of spiritual gifts in Chapter 5, "Rightly Dividing the Word of Truth."

CHAPTER 4 KEY POINTS

- Personal sin interrupts our fellowship with God. It is our responsibility to phone home to restore fellowship with Him. (p. 63)
- Through the grace provision of 1 John 1:9, the Phone Zone (confession of sin), God provides the way to recover fellowship with Him. (p. 64)
- It is impossible to have fellowship with God unless we are empowered by the Spirit. (p. 65)
- We cannot be empowered by the Spirit (Power Zone) apart from 1 John 1:9, the Phone Zone. (p. 66)
- There are no exceptions. (p. 70)
- Recovery from sin must be compatible with at least five grace criteria. (p. 76-77)
- At any given moment after salvation, our soul is either 100 percent controlled by the Spirit or 100 percent controlled by our sin nature. (p. 79)
- Were it not for the power of the Spirit inside the Power Zone, we would have no possibility of victory over our sin nature. (p. 82)

CHAPTER 5: RIGHTLY DIVIDING THE WORD OF TRUTH

Emotional Stability in the Power Zone

> *Gal. 5:22–23 – But the fruit of the Spirit is love, joy, peace, patience, kindness, goodness, faithfulness, gentleness, self-control.*

The words in these verses are important, because the Holy Spirit has everything to do with producing inner peace, patience, self-control, and other qualities that accompany emotional stability. The Holy Spirit has nothing to do with frantic behavior, hyper-emotionalism, or playing "spiritual one-upmanship" with other believers through a self-induced emotional state or by acting out some extinct, temporary spiritual gift. (This chapter will cover temporary gifts)

It is not the purpose of the Holy Spirit to stimulate our emotions. The Holy Spirit is not a switch designed to turn on emotionalism. I can think of a lot of things that might trigger our emotions, but the Spirit is not one of them. If one of the functions of the Spirit is to provide self-control—as in Gal. 5:23—how can it simultaneously provide emotionalism? No believer in the Church Age has ever been more spiritual than any other believer because of the intensity of their response to the music or the message. As we have seen in previous chapters of this book, spirituality is an absolute state of soul provided through grace and without one iota of human merit. Spirituality cannot be enhanced by emotionalism, body posture, body movement, ritual observance, or any system of works. Within limits, it is perfectly legitimate to respond emotionally to music or to a message, but emotional response in any realm of Christianity cannot enhance spirituality.

Besides Gal. 5:22–23, the Apostle Paul tells us in at least four other New Testament passages that emotion is never the measure of spirituality:

> *Phil. 3:18–19 – ... many walk ... as enemies of the cross, whose God is their emotions.*

> *Rom. 10:1–2 – ... my desire for them is for their salvation ... they have emotion for God, but not according to knowledge.*

> *Rom. 16:17–18 – ... note those who cause divisions ... for they don't serve our Lord Jesus Christ, but their own emotions.*

> *2 Cor. 6:11–12 – ... O Corinthians ... you are restricted by your own emotions.*

Paul also had to remind the Corinthians that giving to the church should be based on the believer's grace attitude, not on emotion:

> *2 Cor. 9:7 – Each one accordingly as he has determined in his right lobe, so give, not from distress of mind or compulsion of emotion, for God loves a gracious giver.*

Galatians 5:22–23 tells us that the Spirit provides self-control, and verses 22–23 give us a partial list of the results of the Spirit's power, but it does not tell us how to produce those results.

None of the passages that list the fruits of the Spirit tells us how to produce those results. Therefore, we have to go to other passages to learn how, and therein lies the rub. If your church is not connecting the dots for you between the *how* of Spirit empowerment and the *results* of Spirit empowerment, hopefully this book will stand in the gap. One of the primary purposes of this book is to connect the dots between the how and the results of living in the Power Zone.

It is important to remember that there is nothing we can do outside the Power Zone that is pleasing to God.

> *John 15:5 – ... apart from Me, you can do nothing.*

> *Romans 8:8 – ... those who are in the flesh cannot please God.*

> *John 6:63 – ... it is the Spirit that gives life, the flesh profits nothing ...*

As believers in Christ, anything we do outside the Power Zone is not pleasing to God, because it comes from our sin nature while we are in the soul-status of spiritual death. God is only pleased with our production inside the Power Zone because the power source is the Holy Spirit.

One of the main reasons believers become frustrated in their Christian experience is that they have never learned how to tap into the Power Zone. And how about you? Do you know how to put the power of the Holy Spirit to work in your life? Do you feel adrift, without a rudder, on the stormy seas of the devil's world? If so, then consider:

> *Eph. 4:14 – ... we are no longer to be children, tossed here and there by waves, and carried about by every wind of false doctrine, by the cunning craftiness of deceitful men who lie in wait to deceive.*

It is the power of the Spirit that keeps us from being deceived, and that gives us the discernment, the filters, the power to tell the truth from the lies.

> *1 Cor. 2:5, 10, 12–15 – ... that your faith should not rest on the wisdom of men, but on the power of God. For to us God revealed them through the Spirit; for the Spirit searches all things, even the depths of God.*

Now we have received, not the spirit of the world, but the Spirit who is from God, that we might know the things freely given to us by God, which things we also speak, not in words taught by human wisdom, but in those taught by the Spirit, combining spiritual thoughts with spiritual words. But a natural man does not accept the things of the Spirit of God; for they are foolishness to him, and he cannot understand them, because they are spiritually appraised. But he who is spiritual can discern all things ...

It should be very clear that apart from soul-control by the Spirit inside the Power Zone, man has a thinking problem:

Isaiah 55:8–9 – For My thoughts are not your thoughts, neither are your ways My ways, declares the Lord. For as the heavens are higher than the earth, so are My ways higher than your ways, and My thoughts higher than your thoughts.

And let's remember that we are what we think:

Proverbs 23:7 – For as a man thinks in his right lobe, so he is.

Some believers today apparently think they can produce the results of the Spirit's power through a system of human works. The result of that is, at best, the production of human good through the energy of the flesh; at worst, it is "chain-sinning," loss of blessings in time, and loss of rewards in eternity. For these poor souls, Christianity just doesn't seem to work, because their soul is controlled by their sin nature instead of by the Spirit. Many spend their lives producing human good. They are like football players who can't get in the power position ... like basketball players who can't find the sweet spot ... like baseball pitchers who seldom have the right stuff ... or like pole-vaulters whose pole snaps in the middle of their swing. While the word of God itself never fails, too many Christians today are in "pole snap freefall" because they don't understand the basic fundamentals of spirituality. Many have never learned the full implications of living the Spirit-Directed Life.

Rightly Dividing the Word of Truth at Pentecost

> *1 Cor. 13:11 – When I was a child, I used to speak as a child, think as a child, reason as a child; when I became a man, I did away with childish things.*

> *2 Tim. 2:15 – Study to present yourself approved to God as a workman needing not to be ashamed, rightly dividing the word of truth.*

Because of the unusual events surrounding the Day of Pentecost and the days immediately thereafter, there remains great confusion over such things as the Baptism of the Spirit, spiritual gifts, and the role of Israel in the Church Age. It's amazing what happens when such issues are clarified by rightly dividing the word of truth.

In the period between AD 33 and AD 96, there are at least four inseparably related aftereffects of the cross that can only be understood by rightly dividing the word of truth. All four are directly related to the Power Zone. Diagram 1 should help sort things out:

DIAGRAM 1: Seeing "The Big Picture" Between AD 33 and AD 96

ENDING	BEGINNING	TRANSITION	TRANSFER
First Advent of Christ	Church Age	Spiritual Gifts	Priest Nation
Acts 1:1-9	*Pentecost* / *Rapture*	*Pre-Canon* / *Post-Canon*	*Jews* / *Gentiles*
Acts 2:34-35	*Acts 2* / *1 Thes. 4:16-17*	*1 Cor. 13:8-12* / *1 Cor. 13:8-12*	*Ex. 19:6* / *Mat. 21:43*
Jn. 1:14			*Acts 15:7-15*
			1 Pet. 2:5, 9

In order to understand these four inseparable aftereffects of the cross, let's examine them one at a time:

ENDING ... The first advent of Christ ended when He ascended to the throne room and the Father said to Him:

> *Matt. 22:44 – Sit at My right hand until I make Your enemies Your footstool.*

This most likely marked one of the greatest heavenly celebrations in the history of the universe. It was at this time that Christ gave spiritual gifts to facilitate the formation and perpetuation of the church:

> *Eph. 4:8 – Therefore it says, "When He ascended on high, He led captive a host of captives, and He gave gifts to men."*

It is important to remember that our spiritual gifts are only empowered when we are inside the Power Zone.

BEGINNING ... The Church Age began on the day of Pentecost in the second chapter of Acts and will be terminated at the rapture of the church, 1 Thes. 4:16–17. Prior to the Church Age, the Power Zone was never available to believers. Because Jesus Christ successfully modeled the Power Zone throughout His earthly ministry and throughout six hours on the cross, we are the most privileged recipients of the greatest power system in all of human history.

> *Heb. 8:6 – But now He has obtained a more excellent ministry, by as much as He is also the mediator of a better covenant, which has been enacted on better promises.*

TRANSFER ... Because the Jews repeatedly failed to be stewards of God's word, and because they rejected Christ during His first advent, God transferred priest nation function from the Jews to the Gentiles, Mat. 21: 43. This transfer was extremely important because it occurred with the beginning of the Church Age, in which unprecedented spiritual privileges became available to all believers. Although the universal availability of Spirit empowerment inside the Power Zone is a privilege extended to both Jew and Gentile believers, only Gentile nations can be priest nations to God in the Church Age. The first gentile priest nation was Rome. Rome took over priest nation status from the Jews in August of AD 70 with the destruction of Jerusalem and the temple, as prophesied by Christ in Matt. 24:2:

> *Truly I say to you, not one stone here shall be left upon another, which will not be torn down.*

The fact that there are Jews in Israel and in Jerusalem today has no prophetic meaning for the Church Age. There is no prophecy concerning the Church Age other than its beginning (Isaiah 28: 11-13; Jn. 14:16–17; 16:7; Acts 1:5), that it will be dangerous (Mat. 24:6; 2 Tim. 3:1-7), and that it will end at the Rapture (1 Cor. 15:51–55; Phil. 3:21; 1 Thes. 4:13–18). The Church Age is not an age of prophecy but an age of historical trends, Lk. 21:9. Today it is fruitless to speculate on prophecy, but America's survival as a "priest nation" (see glossary) demands that we take action over historical trends such as Satan's use of religions, peoples, and nations to exterminate Christians and Jews. Biblically speaking, our only protection from this type of evil is decisive military victory, Joshua 11:20 and Psalms 18:38–45.

TRANSITION OF SPIRITUAL GIFTS … Failure to rightly divide the word of truth (2 Tim. 2:15), has sidetracked many believers into distorting scripture, as did the Corinthians of Paul's day. This is especially true where temporary spiritual gifts and the Holy Spirit are concerned. The failure to rightly divide the word of truth has caused great confusion over the role of the Holy Spirit in the Church Age. The Day of Pentecost is a great example. There is so much emotionalism and false doctrine associated with the baptism of the

Holy Spirit and the now-extinct temporary spiritual gifts that these things demand clarification. Before we deal with the transition of spiritual gifts, let's look at the baptism of the Spirit.

Pentecost and the Baptism of the Holy Spirit

The coming of the Holy Spirit to the Apostles on the Day of Pentecost in AD 33 was both a status-bringing event plus an experience. Why was it both? Because it signaled the beginning of the Church Age. God sent the Spirit with a rushing wind and flames of fire in order to impress upon the already saved Apostles that the Church Age had just begun. That was a very important and unusual time in the history of Christianity. After that time, however, for the new believer receiving the Holy Spirit at the moment of salvation it is a status-bringing event only. There are no flames or rushing wind or any other experiential manifestation to indicate the baptism of the Spirit has occurred. The status-bringing event is the Holy Spirit placing the new believer in the top circle, in the Security Zone, in permanent union with Christ forever. This placement into permanent union with Christ is called the Baptism of the Holy Spirit. It is a one-time-event that is neither seen nor felt and has nothing to do with water.

The visible manifestation of the baptism of the Holy Spirit on the day of Pentecost and the temporary spiritual gift of tongues are two separate things. Holy Spirit baptism would have occurred even if the gift of tongues and not been historically necessary. The reason people think they are one and the same is because on the Day of Pentecost, the baptism of the Spirit and the temporary spiritual gift of tongues occurred within a split second of each other. The only thing linking these two different things is that the Holy Spirit is responsible for both. The Baptism of the Holy Spirit is for every believer in Christ in the Church Age, but the temporary spiritual gift of tongues occurred to evangelize dispersed and unbelieving Jews in their own languages.

The baptism of the Holy Spirit continues throughout the Church Age as an unseen and unfelt status-bringing event at the moment of salvation. However, the temporary spiritual gift of tongues came to an abrupt end in August of AD 70 because its purpose had been fulfilled—dispersed and unbelieving Jews had the opportunity to hear the gospel in their own Gentile languages. This evangelization of Jews occurred during a thirty-seven-year grace period prior to the destruction of Jerusalem by the Romans in August of AD 70.

The coming of the Holy Spirit at Pentecost was unusual, to say the least. Imagine being alive on that day described in the second chapter of Acts and witnessing the coming of the Spirit with a rushing wind in flames of fire. Imagine suddenly being able to speak in a language that you did not previously know and that you don't understand even as you speak it. That's why an interpreter was required. In AD 33, few understood that God was using a visible manifestation of the coming of the Spirit plus temporary spiritual gifts to inform them of at least three things:

1. That the Church Age had just begun
2. That the Apostles were chosen by God and had authority over the churches
3. That the Jews would soon be removed as a functioning priest nation and replaced by Gentiles (Mat. 21: 43 and Isaiah 28:11–13, compared with 1 Cor. 14:22a)

Technically, the Jews had long since ceased to be a viable priest nation. However, through the grace of God, Rome had allowed Jerusalem and the Jews the freedom to function as stewards of God's word if they so desired. Few, if any, of the apostate Jerusalem Jews would remember Isaiah's prophesy in Isaiah 28:11–13, that soon after the Jews were evangelized in Gentile languages, their priest nation function would be terminated:

Isa. 28:11–13 – Indeed He will speak to this people through stammering lips and a foreign tongue, He who said to them, "Here is rest, give rest to the

97

weary," and "here is refreshment," but they would not listen ... they may go and stumble backward, be broken, snared, and taken captive. (See also Hosea 4:6.)

Jesus Christ Himself personally told the Jews in Matthew 21:43 that they would lose priest nation function for their failure to accept Him as savior and for failure to be stewards of God's word after centuries of opportunities:

Matt. 21:43 – "Therefore I say to you, the kingdom of God [priest nation function] will be taken away from you, and be given to a nation producing the fruit of it."

What Christ told them would happen did happen, in August of AD 70, when the Romans destroyed Jerusalem and the temple, and Rome became the first Gentile priest nation. You will notice that according to His grace policy, God always gives a period of grace before judgment. Unbelieving Jews had almost forty years to realize what time it was—that God's world clock was now ticking on Gentile time. The Jews who became Christ followers adjusted their clocks to "Gentile-savings time." Unbelieving Jews living in Jerusalem got their clocks cleaned, courtesy of the Romans, and Israel will not serve as a priest nation again until the millennial reign of Christ, Rev. 20:1–6.

In AD 60, Paul told the Romans that in the Church Age, Gentile nations would serve as God's priest nations instead of Israel:

Rom. 11:25 – For I do not want you, believers, to be uniformed of this mystery, lest you be wise in your own estimation, that a partial hardening has happened to Israel until the fullness of the Gentiles has come in ...

By AD 96, Gentile churches and the influence of Christianity had spread all over the Roman world. Directly because of this, humanity entered into perhaps the greatest period of peace and prosperity that the world has ever known, the period of the Antonine Caesars. (For further reading on this era, see the works of Roman historians Edward Gibbon and Theodore Mommsen). While it is not within the scope of this book to cover the details of that period, failure to credit the positive influence of Christianity on that era would be the worst form of blasphemy.

The Gift of Tongues and Other Temporary Spiritual Gifts

In 1 Cor. 14:21, the Apostle Paul repeated Isaiah's prophecy of tongues, as a warning to the Jews. Then, in verse 22, Paul reminds them of the purpose of the gift of tongues:

> *1 Cor. 14:22 – So then tongues are for a sign, not to those who believe, but to unbelievers.*

The purpose of tongues (Jews being evangelized in Gentile languages) was to warn unbelieving Jews that since they had rejected Christ and failed over time to be stewards of God's word, they would soon be removed as a functioning priest nation. Because of the Jews' repeated failures to please God, they had been dispersed on several previous occasions as part of God's cycles of discipline of the Jews.

> *Levit. 26:27, 33 – Yet in spite of this [previous cycles of discipline], if you do not obey Me, but act with hostility against Me ... I will scatter you among the nations and draw out a sword after you, as your land becomes desolate and your cities become waste.*

Total military defeat and resultant dispersion was the fifth and final cycle of discipline. For details on all five cycles, refer to Lev. 26:14–39. The fact that the Jews as a nation were still under dispersion discipline during the age of the Apostles is obvious in

Acts 2:7–11 and in James's opening address to the Jews in James 1:1:

> *James, a bond-servant of God and of the Lord Jesus Christ, to the twelve tribes who are dispersed abroad, greetings.*

Having been dispersed by God for generations, the Jews spoke the Gentile language of their geographical location. Therefore, they needed to hear the gospel of Christ in their own native Gentile language. This required the temporary spiritual gift of tongues to evangelize unbelieving Jews who had congregated in Jerusalem in AD 33 in the presence of the Apostles. Because of God's policy of grace before judgment, dispersed and unbelieving Jews had roughly forty years after the resurrection of Christ to change their mind about the reality of the cross.

As evidenced by their attempts to kill the Apostle Paul in Acts 23, Jewish apostasy was centered in Jerusalem. Therefore, the demonstration of God's discipline to the Jews was focused in that city. As previously mentioned, this Divine discipline culminated in August of AD 70, when Jerusalem and the temple were destroyed. From that date forward, long before the canon of scripture was completed in AD 96, tongues had been removed as a temporary spiritual gift. Why? Because the purpose of tongues as a warning to unbelieving Jews had been realized. That's why Paul told the Corinthians in AD 59 that the entire category of temporary spiritual gifts would be eliminated as soon as the purpose for each had been fulfilled:

> *1 Cor. 13:8 – ... if there are gifts of prophecy, they will be done away; if there are tongues, they will cease; if there is knowledge, it will be done away.*

While verse 8 is categorical instead of a complete list, Paul makes it very clear in 1 Cor. 13:8–12 that all temporary spiritual gifts will cease categorically, including the following:

- prophesy
- tongues
- knowledge of scripture prior to its insertion into the canon

Other Apostolic temporary spiritual gifts that would cease by AD 96 are:

- miracles
- healing
- interpretation of tongues

God still performs miracles and heals infirmities, but instead of using intermediaries, such as the Apostles, who needed to establish their authenticity and their authority over the newborn churches, He does it personally. God can and does heal, perform miracles, etc., but it's God's power, with limited human involvement other than intercessory prayer and self-petition. All Apostolic spiritual gifts ended with the death of John, the last Apostle, Rev. 2:2.

Temporary spiritual gifts must be placed within their proper historical setting in which they helped the Apostles gain both an audience and credibility. By AD 96, when the canon was completed and being circulated, the temporary spiritual gifts had been totally phased out. For example, the Apostle Paul—after bringing Eutychus back to life at Troy, in AD 59—was unable to heal his friends Epaphroditus in AD 64 and Trophimus in AD 66, as referenced by Acts 20:10, Phil. 2:25–27, and 2 Tim. 4:20.

Concerning the temporary spiritual gift of tongues, nowhere in the New Testament does it indicate that gift was operational at any time after AD 70. It just isn't there. Even when it was operational, Paul listed the gift of tongues as being the least of all temporary gifts, in 1 Cor. 12: 28. Why? As a former Pharisee and an expert in the Old Testament, Paul simply restated Isaiah's prophesy of Isaiah 28:11–13, that tongues was a "sign," a warning, to unbelieving Jews, 1 Cor.14:21–22. He knew that the temporary spiritual gift of tongues would be phased out as soon as its purpose was fulfilled.

After AD 70, the purpose of tongues as a warning to unbelieving Jews had been fulfilled, and therefore the gift of tongues and the interpretation of tongues became obsolete. The gift of tongues was never for believing Gentiles, it was for unbelieving Jews, which the Bible makes clear in 1 Cor. 14:22.

In 1 Cor. 13: 8, the type of prophecy gift that God removed is best described by the term "foretelling," the telling of what is going to happen before it happens. The other type of prophecy is called "forth-telling," which simply means to communicate what the word of God says. Unfortunately, some people still think that prophecy—as in foretelling—is still operational today. The word of God through the Apostle Paul says otherwise.

The Apostle John made evident in Rev. 2: 1–2 that the temporary spiritual gift and office of "Apostle" was the last temporary gift to exist. John is writing as directed by Christ to the church in Ephesus, the new center of Christianity after Jerusalem was destroyed. He is commending the church for having the spiritual wisdom to realize the he, John, was the last living Apostle and that this temporary gift and office would cease with his death:

> *To the angel [pastor] of the church in Ephesus ...*
> *"I know your deeds and your toil and perseverance,*
> *and that you cannot endure evil men, and you put to*
> *the test those who call themselves apostles, and they*
> *are not, and you found them liars."*

The gift and office of Apostle is no longer operational for at least three reasons:

1. Apostolic authority over multiple and newly founded churches was required only until the Bible was completed and being circulated.
2. Protection is still required for the autonomous local Christian church in every nation from the collective false doctrines of those who want to dictate message content to the individual

pastors of local churches. That is the realm of the Holy Spirit, not another pastor.

3. In the Church Age, every believer is a priest, 1 Pet. 2:5, 9. This means that regardless of the believer's spiritual gift, no believer has a special "in" with God. At any given moment after salvation, all believers are either in or out of fellowship with God, dependent upon confession, regardless of their spiritual gift.

Thanks to Jesus Christ, every believer has equal access to God through the grace provision of the Power Zone. Any believer functioning in the Power Zone, regardless of his or her spiritual gift, is just as much empowered by the Spirit as any other believer. Spirituality is an absolute state of soul that is not improved by a spiritual gift, regardless of the authority attached to the gift. For example, the gift of pastor-teacher does not make the pastor more spiritual than members of the congregation with, for example, the gift of hospitality. At any given moment they are both either spiritual, or carnal, regardless of the spiritual gift they possess. When we are out of fellowship with God because of sin, we still possess our spiritual gifts; we are simply not empowered by the Spirit to use them. Obviously, in order for our spiritual gift to function at full capacity, spiritual growth plus Spirit soul-control is required. Spirit soul-control can't occur unless we are inside the Power Zone in fellowship with God.

In the Church Age, each pastor is directly responsible before God for the spiritual growth of his own autonomous local church. Other than God and His word, there is no higher spiritual authority than the pastor of the local church. A pastor does not have the apostolic authority to dictate the messages to the pastor of another local church or group of churches. However, this does not prohibit a pastor from delivering a message from a central campus to one or more satellite campuses. For the Church Age, the permanent spiritual gift of pastor-teacher has replaced the extinct temporary spiritual gift of Apostle. The fact that there are religious sects violating this doctrine today only proves that apostasy continues throughout the Church Age. It is humankind, not God, that has put men in dictatorial positions over wide-reaching religious sects and given them titles.

Not only does God desire autonomous local churches, He also desires separate, independent, and sovereign nations who protect their freedoms, borders, and common cultural heritage.

> *Acts 17:26–27 – And He made from one, every nation of mankind to live on all the face of the earth, having determined their appointed times and the boundaries of their habitation, that they should seek God.*

The purpose of sovereign nations is so humankind might seek God. The father of United Nations–style internationalism is Satan, not God. God has taken at least two steps to isolate evil in the Church Age: creating sovereign nations and creating sovereign local churches. Leave it to the collective sin natures of man to organize and rebel against Divine design.

Keep in mind that the temporary gifts were not all removed at the same time; they were phased out over a period of roughly sixty years. The gift of tongues (a believer evangelizing unbelievers in the unbelievers' language) was among the first to be removed, and it never has been the same thing as the Baptism of the Holy Spirit. Spirit baptism is a one-time event that occurs at the moment of salvation, when the Holy Spirit puts the new believer into permanent union with Christ in the Security Zone. Today, Spirit baptism is not an experience—it is not a feeling. The only reason we know it occurs is because the Bible tells us it does, in passages like 1 Cor. 12:13:

> *For by one Spirit we are all baptized into one body, whether Jews or Gentiles, bond or free.*

Because the beginning of the Church Age was surrounded by unusual events, there was and is a great deal of confusion over the role of the Spirit and the phasing out of temporary spiritual gifts. Unlike the believers of Acts 2, we have the benefit of the completed canon of scripture. Those willing to rightly divide the word of truth and those willing to hear the truth know exactly what the role of the Spirit is in the Church Age. We also know by comparing and contrasting scriptures the temporary spiritual gifts that were phased out and the permanent spiritual gifts that were phased in between AD 33 and AD 96. There was so much confusion over the phasing out and phasing in of spiritual gifts in the early church that the Apostle Paul took no fewer than three chapters—1 Cor. 12–14—to get believers straightened out on these matters. Some believers didn't understand then, and some still don't understand now. Perhaps a section from diagram 1 shown in greater detail will help.

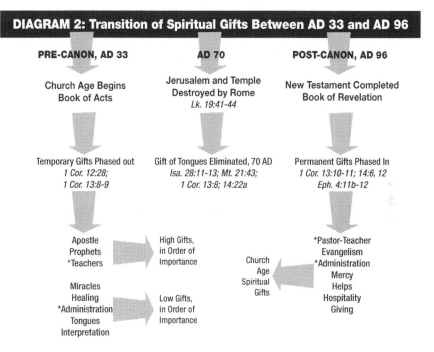

DIAGRAM 2: Transition of Spiritual Gifts Between AD 33 and AD 96

PRE-CANON, AD 33

Church Age Begins
Book of Acts

Temporary Gifts Phased out
1 Cor. 12:28;
1 Cor. 13:8-9

Apostle
Prophets
*Teachers

Miracles
Healing
*Administration
Tongues
Interpretation

AD 70

Jerusalem and Temple
Destroyed by Rome
Lk. 19:41-44

Gift of Tongues Eliminated, 70 AD
Isa. 28:11-13; Mt. 21:43;
1 Cor. 13:8; 14:22a

High Gifts,
in Order of
Importance

Low Gifts,
in Order of
Importance

Church
Age
Spiritual
Gifts

POST-CANON, AD 96

New Testament Completed
Book of Revelation

Permanent Gifts Phased In
1 Cor. 13:10-11; 14:6, 12
Eph. 4:11b-12

*Pastor-Teacher
Evangelism
*Administration
Mercy
Helps
Hospitality
Giving

It is important to remember that the temporary gifts were phased out over time between AD 33 and AD 96. Notice that there are two carry-over gifts—teachers and administration—because the early churches required teachers and administration, just as today's churches do. Also be aware that the list of permanent gifts in diagram 2 is by no means an exhaustive list, although it is likely that some of the other gifts that might be included fit into one of the categories listed.

Bringing 1 Cor. 13:8–12 into the Light

1 Cor. 13:8–12 is very important because in verse 8, Paul says that temporary spiritual gifts will end as a category, and in verses 9–12 he tells us when they will end. In this passage, Paul is contrasting at least two different things: (1) pre-canon temporary spiritual gifts with post-canon permanent spiritual gifts, and (2) pre-canon with post-canon knowledge of scripture:

> *V 9 – for we know in part and we prophesy in part [New Testament not complete] ...*

> *V 10 – but when the perfect comes [completed New Testament], the partial shall be done away [temporary spiritual gifts] ...*

> *V 11 – When I was a child, I spoke as a child, thought as a child, reasoned as a child [pre-canon knowledge was incomplete and gifts were different (see diagram 2)]; when I became a man, I did away with childish things [temporary spiritual gifts obsolete when the Bible is complete].*

> *V 12 – For now we see through a mirror dimly ... now I know in part [New Testament incomplete, temporary gifts needed] ... but then face to face ... I shall know fully [Bible complete, temporary gifts replaced with better, permanent gifts] ...*

In verse 10 it is critically important to know that "the perfect" refers to the AD 96 completion of the New Testament. It cannot refer to the first or second coming of Jesus Christ for five reasons:

1. "The perfect" is the translation of the Greek word *teleios*, meaning "to complete." Christ's work was completed in AD 33 when He said, "It is finished," so "when the perfect comes" cannot refer to Christ. It refers to the completion of the New Testament in AD 96.

2. "The perfect" is in the neuter gender; if it referred to the first or second coming of Christ, it would be in the masculine gender. "The perfect" refers to an "it," not a "him," and therefore refers to the future completion of the New Testament.

3. This passage, including the phrase "when the perfect comes," was written in AD 59, after which, obviously, Christ had already come.

4. Verse 10 says "when the perfect comes, the partial will be done away." The only thing "the partial" can refer to is temporary spiritual gifts. It can't be Christ or the Bible.

5. Verse 12 tells us that "when the perfect comes" we will "know fully," but until then we will only "see through a mirror dimly."

If "the perfect" referred to the second coming of Christ, then we would remain in the dark, seeing "through a mirror dimly," until the second advent of Christ. Very few Christians would believe that God has left us in the dark now for over two thousand years. If God wanted us to remain in the dark until the second coming of Christ, He wouldn't have sent His Son as "the light of the world":

> *John 8:12 – ... I am the light of the world; he who follows me shall not walk in the darkness, but shall have the light of life.*

If God wanted to keep us in the dark, He wouldn't have given us the New Testament, revealing all the mystery doctrines of the Church Age:

> *Eph. 3:8–9 – To me [Paul], the least of all believers, this grace was given, to preach to the Gentiles the unfathomable riches of Christ, and to bring to light what is the administration of the mystery [Church Age] which for ages has been hidden in God ...*

If God wanted to keep us in the dark, we wouldn't have the universal indwelling and empowerment of the Spirit:

> *Gal. 5:25 – If we live by the Spirit [indwelling], let us also walk by the Spirit [Power].*

If God wanted to keep us in the dark, we wouldn't have all the ministries of the Spirit available to us inside the Power Zone:

> *2 Tim. 1:7; Rom. 15:13 – ... God has not given us a Spirit of weakness, but of power ... that you may abound in hope by the power of the Holy Spirit.*

If God wanted us to remain in the dark, He wouldn't have given us the mind of His Son in writing, the completed canon of scripture:

> *1 Cor. 2:16 – For who has known the mind of the Lord, that we should instruct Him. But we have the mind of Christ.*

If God wanted us to remain in the dark, He would not command us to walk in the light:

> *Eph. 5:8 – ... now you are light in the Lord; walk as children of light [in the Power Zone].*

In John 16:12–15, Jesus Himself verified that we would not remain in the dark when He told the Disciples that the Spirit would reveal to them "all the truth" and "all things" that Church Age believers would need to know as the soon-to-be Apostles completed the canon of scripture.

At this point a couple of summaries should be helpful:

Reasons for Temporary Spiritual Gifts between AD 33 and AD 96

1. To warn unbelieving Jews to reconsider the cross and that priest nation function would be terminated: Isa. 28:11–13; 1 Cor. 13:8–12; Matt. 21:43; Acts 13:46; Rom. 11:17, 25.

2. To present the gospel to unbelieving Jews in their own languages: Acts 2:5–10; 1 Cor. 14:22.

3. To gain the Apostles a hearing: Rom. 11:25; Eph. 3:8; Col. 1:27.

4. To bring into remembrance the spoken words of Christ so that the New Testament could be written by the Apostles and circulated to the churches: Jn. 14:26; 16:12–15; Eph. 3:1–10; Col. 1:25–27.

5. To establish infant churches and train their new pastors: Acts 6:2–7; 20:17, 28.

Why Temporary Spiritual Gifts Were Phased Out between AD 33 and AD 96

1. The gift of tongues was removed in August of AD 70 because its purpose as a warning to unbelieving Jews had been met. See points 1 and 2, first summary.

2. The spectacular but temporary gifts had been distorted to distraction, 1 Cor. 12:28–14:28. Paul wrote three chapters to the Corinthians to straighten out the distortions.

3. Paul made it clear that when the New Testament was completed and the first churches were established that the temporary gifts would be terminated because they were no longer needed, 1 Cor. 13:8–12.

4. Now that we have the mind of Christ in writing, we have a more excellent way: 1 Cor. 2:16; 12:31.

5. Because Christ successfully modeled the Power Zone all the way through His ministry and throughout six hours on the cross, we have something unprecedented in human history: a more excellent ministry, a better covenant, and better promises, Heb. 8:6.

6. Therefore, pre-canon temporary spiritual gifts are now obsolete, having been replaced by superior post-canon Divine operating assets for all believers, such as permanent spiritual gifts, the universal priesthood, the universal indwelling of the Spirit, and the universal availability of the Power Zone.

If we are going to take advantage of our superior Divine operating assets, including our spiritual gifts, we need to understand the importance of staying out of the spiritual death zones. In Chapter 6, we will take a close look at the first spiritual death zone, "The Clone Zone."

CHAPTER 5 KEY POINTS

- The Holy Spirit has everything to do with producing inner peace, self-control, and other qualities that accompany emotional stability. (p. 89)
- Emotional response in any realm of Christianity cannot enhance spirituality. (p. 89)
- Because of the unusual events surrounding the Day of Pentecost, there remains great confusion over the Baptism of the Spirit, spiritual gifts, and the role of Israel in the Church Age. (p. 93)
- Placement into permanent union with Christ is called the Baptism of the Holy Spirit. It is a one-time status-bringing event that is neither seen nor felt and has nothing to do with water. (p. 96)
- The purpose of tongues was to warn unbelieving Jews that since they had rejected Christ and failed to be stewards of God's word, they would soon be removed as a functioning priest nation. (p. 99)
- Temporary spiritual gifts must be placed within their proper historical setting, in which they helped the Apostles gain both an audience and credibility. (p. 101)
- In 1 Cor. 13:8, Paul says temporary spiritual gifts will end as a category, and in verses 9–12 he tells us when they will end. (p. 106)
- There are 5 reasons for temporary spiritual gifts between AD 33 and AD 96. (p. 109)
- There are 6 reasons why temporary spiritual gifts were phased out by AD 96. (p. 109-110)

CHAPTER 6: THE CLONE ZONE

Walking Like Mere Men

Before salvation, our only soul-control power source was our sin nature. After salvation, we have the grace option of living in the Power Zone and being empowered by the Spirit. However, we still retain our resident sin nature after salvation. When we choose to sin, we lose Spirit empowerment and switch our power source from the Spirit back to our old sin nature. Therefore, any act of sin means that we have *cloned ourselves* back under the only power we knew as unbelievers, our sin nature. Our decision to sin causes loss of fellowship with God and loss of empowerment by the Spirit. The instant we choose to step out of the Power Zone through personal sin, we are imitating the unbeliever and walking like mere men, 1 Cor. 3: 3. The only way to return to the Power Zone is through the grace provision of 1 John 1:9, confession of sin.

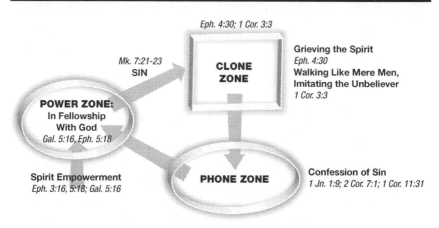

DIAGRAM 1: Walking Like Mere Men

Eph. 4:30; 1 Cor. 3:3

CLONE ZONE

Grieving the Spirit
Eph. 4:30
Walking Like Mere Men, Imitating the Unbeliever
1 Cor. 3:3

Mk. 7:21-23
SIN

POWER ZONE:
In Fellowship With God
Gal. 5:16, Eph. 5:18

Spirit Empowerment
Eph. 3:16, 5:18; Gal. 5:16

PHONE ZONE

Confession of Sin
1 Jn. 1:9; 2 Cor. 7:1; 1 Cor. 11:31

When we commit an act of sin and enter the first stage of spiritual death, the Clone Zone, 1 Cor. 3:3 calls this "walking like mere men." Not only are we commanded not to do this, we are compared to animals if it becomes our lifestyle:

> *Eph. 4:22 – That in reference to your former manner of life, you lay aside the old self, which is being corrupted in accordance with the lusts of deceit ...*

> *1 Cor. 3:3 – for you are still carnal [out of the Power Zone]. For since there is jealousy and strife among you, are you not carnal, and are you not walking like mere men [like an unbeliever]?*

> *1 Pet. 1:14 – As obedient children, do not be conformed to the former lusts which were yours in your ignorance.*

> *2 Pet. 2:22 – It has happened to them according to the true proverb, "A dog returns to its own vomit," and "a sow, after washing, returns to wallowing in the mire."*

It is very important to remember that any category of sin defiles us before God (makes us unclean). How do we know that? Remember that Jesus Christ Himself tells us so in Mark 7:20–23:

> *"That which proceeds out of the man, that is what defiles the man. For from within, out of the heart of men, proceed the evil thoughts and fornications, thefts, murders, adulteries, deeds of coveting and wickedness, as well as deceit, sensuality, envy, slander, pride and foolishness. All these things proceed from within and defile the man."*

Some reminders about the results of sin are important here. Remember that when we first decide to sin, we lose fellowship with God and we lose the empowerment of the Spirit, because we are grieving the Spirit in the Clone Zone. When we fail to confess sin, we degenerate into the Groan Zone, where we quench the Spirit. We are warned not to do either one.

> *Eph. 4:30 – ... do not grieve the Holy Spirit*
> *1 Thes. 5:19 – Do not quench the Spirit*

And let's not forget that being out of the Power Zone because of sin means that we are spiritually dead and separated from God because of uncleanness:

> *Rom. 6:23 – ... the wages of sin is death ...*
> *Jm. 2:26 – ... the body without the Spirit is dead ...*

God never intends that we remain unclean and therefore gives us the grace provision of confession of sin to bring us back into the Power Zone and under the control of the Holy Spirit:

> *1 John 1:9 – If we confess our sins, He is faithful and righteous to forgive us our sins and to cleanse us from all unrighteousness.*

> *1 Cor. 11:31 – But if we judge ourselves rightly, we should not be judged.*

> *2 Cor. 7:1 – Therefore having these promises, believers, let us cleanse ourselves from all defilement of flesh and spirit, perfecting holiness in the fear of God.*

Personal Enemy No. 1: We Choose Our Own Soul-Control

In this chapter, we're going to see what happens to us when sin takes us out of fellowship with God, out of the Power Zone, and places us under the control of our sin nature. As long as we fail to confess sin directly to God, we remain under the control of sin. It always pays to know our enemy—and our greatest enemy resides within us. We might as well go look at ourselves in the mirror and say, "Hello personal enemy number one!" The issue is who controls our soul. The only way we can win the soul-control battle is to be in fellowship with God inside the Power Zone. Fellowship with God occurs only in the Power Zone, where the Spirit defeats our weaknesses while developing our human strengths and spiritual gifts to the glory of God.

Never forget that it is our own freewill decisions (James 1:13–15) that cause our sin nature to rule our lives.

> *Let no one say when he is tempted, "I am being tempted by God"; for God cannot be tempted by evil, and He Himself does not tempt anyone. But each one is tempted when he is carried away and enticed by his own lust. Then when lust has conceived, it gives birth to sin; and when sin is accomplished it brings forth spiritual death.*

In other words, we choose our system of soul-control. We either choose God's system or we choose Satan's system. We either choose to be controlled by the Holy Spirit inside the Power Zone, or we choose to be controlled by our sin nature outside the Power Zone. Once we get out of fellowship with God by choosing to sin, we open the door to all areas of lust, plus self-denial and human good.

Choosing to sin is very similar to the choice that Adam had in the Garden. His choice was God inside the Garden or Eve outside the Garden. We know what choice he made, and here we are. Apparently, Adam was so in love with Eve, it never occurred to him that God could have provided him with another woman inside the Garden. Since Adam made the wrong choice, every human baby is contaminated by Adam's sin. After salvation, we choose either to be inside the Power Zone or outside of it through sin.

Sin comes in three categories: mental, verbal, and overt—in other words, what we think, what we say, and what we do. By far, the worst category of sin falls under the category of what we think, because it is what we think that determines what we say and do. There is no such thing as a verbal or overt sin that was not first a thought.

The greatest challenge in the Christian life is soul-control, which is determined by our thought pattern. Remember Prov. 23:7: As a man thinks in his right lobe, so he is. In the Bible the word "heart" refers to the right lobe of the brain, because that's where our values reside. When God evaluates believers, guess where He looks?

> *1 Sam. 16:7 – ... man looks at the outward appearance, but God looks at the heart.*

Sin is the worst problem we're ever going to face, because it takes us out of the Power Zone into a soul status of spiritual death. If this state of soul is perpetuated, then all spiritual death stages become possible. Let's remember that God gave us the Power Zone for at least five reasons: fellowship with Him, empowerment, growth, production, and effective prayer. God has ensured that these things work synergistically, with the ultimate objective of developing the mind of Christ in our right lobes.

> *Phil. 2:5; Rom. 12:2 – Let this mind be in you that was in Christ Jesus ... be transformed by the renewing of your mind*

We are commanded to live in the Power Zone in order to avoid sin and to make Christ's values our own.

> *Eph. 3:16–17 – ... be strengthened with power through His Spirit in the inner man, so that Christ may dwell in your hearts ...*

Since the word of God has been the mind of Christ from the very beginning, it is the standard by which God evaluates us as believers.

John 1:1 – In the beginning, which was not a beginning, in eternity past, was the Word. And the Word was with God, and the Word was God [Jesus Christ].

1 Cor. 2:16 – ... we have the mind of Christ [the Bible is the mind of Christ in writing].

Heb. 4:12 – For the word of God ... is able to judge the thoughts and intents of the heart.

A Closer Look at Our Sin Nature

Being in the Clone Zone simply means being in the first zone of spiritual death or the first zone in sin nature soul-control. Before we look at our sin nature in greater detail, we will need to be able to refer to the sin nature diagram.

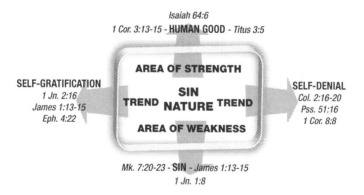

DIAGRAM 2: The Four Categories of Sin Nature Production

Isaiah 64:6
1 Cor. 3:13-15 - HUMAN GOOD *- Titus 3:5*

AREA OF STRENGTH

SELF-GRATIFICATION
1 Jn. 2:16
James 1:13-15
Eph. 4:22

SIN
TREND NATURE TREND

SELF-DENIAL
Col. 2:16-20
Pss. 51:16
1 Cor. 8:8

AREA OF WEAKNESS

Mk. 7:20-23 - SIN *- James 1:13-15*
1 Jn. 1:8

In all zones of spiritual death the sin nature rules our soul, so the Clone Zone is the logical place to examine each of the four categories of sin nature production. Let's start with self-gratification. In all three of the passages under self-gratification, the issue is lust. Self-gratification means that we are chasing one or more of the trends in our own personal lust pattern. Therefore, from this point forward I will substitute the word "lust" for self-gratification simply because it is an easier term to work with.

Sin and lust are easy to understand, and they are very closely related. However, lusts are so powerful that they are classified separately. There are all types of lust. Some examples include the following:

- power lust
- lust for approbation (attention)
- money lust
- lust for things money can buy (materialism lust)
- sex lust
- chemical dependency
- party lust
- wanderlust

Even emotional stimulation of all types can be included. The object of our lust may not be a sin in and of itself—it is the obsession to possess or to be consumed by the area of our lust that is the problem. For example, money is not evil in itself, but ...

> *1 Tim. 6:10 – ... the love of money is the root of all types of evil ...*

When Satan persuaded Adam and Eve to join him in sin, he introduced humankind to what I call his coins of cosmic currency. When we are controlled by our sin nature and being "cosmic Christians", we are out in *cosmos diabolicus* (the devil's world) spending Satan's coins. This is just another way of saying that we are controlled by our sin nature. Satan has more than two coins, but for the sake of simplicity, in this book we are only going to examine two of them. The first coin we'll call "cosmic chaos." It has sin on one side and lust on the other:

DIAGRAM 3: Satan's Coin for Cosmic Chaos

SIN   **LUST**

Remember that when we are out of fellowship with God through sin, there are two different trends we may follow. Self-denial is one trend, while self-gratification or lust is the other. Right now we are dealing with the lust trend. Lusts are always insatiable; once we begin to feed our lust trends, they demand more and more, until they destroy our spiritual life.

Satan's downfall was lust for power and approbation, motivated by pride and arrogance, Isa. 14:12–14. If lust destroyed Satan, who is much more powerful than we are, how can we as mere mortals expect to survive by chasing one or more of our lust trends? Since Satan knows what our personal lust trends are, he tempts us in our areas of weakness, where we are most prone to sin. We are commanded to stop catering to our areas of weakness:

> *Heb. 12:1 – ... let us lay also lay aside every weight, and the sin which so easily entangles us, and let us run with endurance the race that is set before us.*

The only way we can consistently resist these temptations to sin is by keeping short accounts with God through confession while advancing to spiritual maturity. This requires the daily intake of the word of God over an extended period. If we win the battle over sin and lust, Satan has yet another coin of cosmic currency up his sleeve.

DIAGRAM 4: Satan's Coin for Counterfeit Spirituality

SELF-DENIAL  **HUMAN GOOD**

Satan's coin of counterfeit spirituality has self-denial on one side and human good on the other. Let's look at self-denial first.

Self-denial is the concept of trying to impress God or people by giving things up for God. We do not become more spiritual by denying ourselves anything that is perfectly legitimate. Self-denial describes the lifestyle of the "holier-than-thou" religious crowd, constantly trying to earn brownie points with God through sacrifice. Christ Himself warned us about these types in Matthew 23:27, when He called the scribes and Pharisees "white-washed tombstones" ... outside, beautiful, but inside full of dead men's bones. These religious Jews were still clinging to the sacrificial life under the Mosaic Law, assuming they were spiritual by doing so, while totally rejecting the grace message of Christ. In Psalms 51:16–17, David tells us that God does not require sacrifices but a changed heart.

> *For You do not delight in sacrifice, otherwise I would give it ... a broken and contrite heart, O God, You will not despise.*

After Christ's death and resurrection, the religious Jews were warned by the author of Hebrews to stop practicing the sacrificial life of the Mosaic Law, because Christ had provided something better:

> *Heb. 8:6 – But now He has obtained a more excellent ministry, by as much as He is also the mediator of a better covenant, which has been enacted on better promises.*

Paul reminded the Colossians that the Church Age is not the age of spirituality by ritualistic observances, food taboos, or by any other system of denying self of non-sinful things:

> *Col. 2:16,18,20–21 – Therefore let no one act as your judge in regard to food or drink or in respect to a festival or a new moon or a Sabbath day ... Let no on keep defrauding you of your prize by delighting in self-abasement [self-denial] ... If you have died with Christ [Security Zone] to the elementary principles of the world, why, as if you were living in the world [out of the Power Zone], do you submit yourself to decrees, such as, "Do not handle, do not taste, do not touch!"*

> *1 Cor. 8:8 – But food will not commend us to God; we are neither the worse if we do not eat, nor the better if we do eat.*

Paul is trying to make it clear that self-denial of non-sinful things does not make a believer spiritual. Anytime God wants us to stop doing something, He has several options or combinations of options. For example, He will motivate us through His Spirit inside the Power Zone, or if we are in a sinful zone, He might discipline us so severely we will think twice before committing the sin again. Self-denial is motivated by our sin nature; therefore, the motivation is always for the wrong reasons. Believers thus motivated actually believe God is impressed with their hard work and sacrifice. Nonsense! God is only impressed by what we produce while under the Spirit's power. When we are in the Power Zone, it is the Holy Spirit providing the power and motivation for our actions, and therefore human merit can never be claimed. When we are in the Power Zone, the glory goes where it belongs: to God.

The Huge Issue of Human Good

Human good is a huge issue in the Christian life because it is made up of the highly visible good deeds that we produce while we are out of fellowship with God. As you can see in diagram 2, the sin nature does not just produce sin, self-gratification, and self-denial, it also produces human good. Human good is the other side of the coin of self-denial. God makes it very clear what He thinks about human good:

> *Isaiah 64:6 – For all of us have become like one who is unclean, and all our righteous deeds are like a filthy rag.*

Human good is different from self-denial. Self-denial is trying to impress God and others by what we are not doing, by things we are giving up. Human good is trying to impress God and others by what we *are* doing. It should be obvious that the same person could be trying to use both false systems to impress God or man.

One of the major problems in modern Christianity is that so many Christians assume that because they are "being good," they are spiritual. Substituting a clean, moral lifestyle for living in the Power Zone is one of the most misguided acts among believers today. Spirituality is not a lifestyle. It isn't a system of good deeds or behavior patterns. It isn't regular church attendance, serving in a church ministry, or volunteering in the mission field. Spirituality is not giving things up for God or changing your lifestyle for God. Spirituality is not fasting or donating your money to the church. Spirituality is not a relative state of soul, it is an absolute state of soul. Spirituality does not come in degrees, depending on how emotionally stimulated, moral, nice, sweet, helpful, and thoughtful you are, or how many Bible verses you can memorize.

If there is anything that will fool today's Christians into believing that they are "spiritual," it is the things I just mentioned. What is the problem? The problem is that it isn't the doing of those things that makes us spiritual. The problem is that all the things I just mentioned can be done by the unbeliever or by the believer out of fellowship. If accomplished when out of fellowship, good deeds are classified by God as human good. Believers awash in human good are usually the ones claiming to be the most spiritual. Let's remember what spirituality actually is, from chapter 1: spirituality is the absolute state of soul-control by the Holy Spirit.

Spirituality is living inside the Power Zone, in the bottom circle, in fellowship with God, receiving power, motivation, and direction from the Holy Spirit. The Spirit-directed believer is the guided missile, the "weapon of mass instruction" that Satan can't handle or duplicate. Because Satan cannot control us as Spirit-directed, moral believers, he will attempt to distract us with human good, self-denial, morality, or emotionalism and try to get us spiritually off track through his multifaceted, counterattack system.

Satan has recruited some of the most persuasive, dynamic, talented, articulate, entertaining, and attractive sales reps on the planet. A few of them operate out of churches. Many of them operate from elected public offices and are constantly promoted by the mass media. Satan uses his recruits to keep Christians so busy producing human good and chasing pseudo-spirituality that they don't have the time to grow up spiritually. Why should we expect this from Satan? Because the first thing he ever did to attack man was to invade the Garden and deceive the woman into believing that she could be as good as God and smarter than Adam if she would just eat of the tree. Human good is Satan's way of deceiving us into believing that we are spiritual, when in fact we are carnal. Human good is like taking certain kinds of drugs, because it makes us think that everything is absolutely rosy, when in reality things are pathetic and we are completely out of fellowship with God.

Satan promotes human good and emotionalism because it makes believers feel good. But spirituality has nothing to do with how you feel. In a church praise service—providing both of the following are in fellowship with God—the mute quadriplegic in the wheelchair is just as spiritual as the believer jumping up and down screaming, "Jesus!" If self-expression made us spiritual, does that mean the believer who can't move or speak a word can never be spiritual? How absurd! Self-expression, body movement, body posture, or how you feel have nothing to do with being spiritual. Believers can be spiritual while being terminally ill and feeling horrible. The last thing Satan wants is for us to be under the direction of an effective power, regardless of self-expression or how we feel.

Never forget that human good is produced by the sin nature's area of strength. There is only one power stronger than our sin nature: the power of the Holy Spirit:

> *1 John 4:4 – Greater is He that is in you than he that is in the world.*

And woe unto the poor souls who are deceived into believing they can make up their sins to God, either through a system of penance or through a system of human good. These are the unfortunate souls who do not have the power to avoid sin, because they remain out of the Power Zone, due to their failure to confess sin. Instead of confessing sin, they try to make their sins up to God through penance, or human good, or both. This type of believer is perfectly described in James 1:8:

> *... a double-minded man, unstable in all his ways.*

Why are they "double-minded"? Go back to the two coins of cosmic currency. They are using either the cosmic chaos coin or the counterfeit spirituality coin, and obviously these coins have two sides—in other words, double-sided equals double-minded! In a previous chapter, we called these types of believers "dipsticks." And why are these dipstick-believers unstable? They are unstable because their life is flipping back and forth between the two coins. They use Satan's cosmic currency to spend their way into spiritual bankruptcy, and all the time Satan is laughing with sadistic glee, while the Spirit's power remains untapped. It should be obvious, then, that Satan has a two-pronged attack on the human race:

DIAGRAM 5: Satan's Two-Pronged Attack

COSMIC CHAOS

Sin and Lust

COUNTERFEIT SPIRITUALITY

Human Good and Self-Denial

As we continue to concentrate on the issue of human good, we can see that the word of God makes it very clear that human good was rejected at the cross:

Eph. 2:8–9 – For by grace you have been saved through faith; and that not of yourselves, it is the gift of God, not of works, lest any man should boast.

2 Tim. 1:8–9 – ... the power of God ... saved us ... not according to our works, but according to His own purpose and grace ...

Titus 3:5 – He saved us not on the basis of deeds which we have done in righteousness, but according to His mercy ...

If God rejected human good for salvation, why would anyone think He accepts human good for spirituality after salvation? Human good is produced by our sin nature in the soul status of spiritual death and therefore can't even be related to spirituality.

Christ Teaches the Difference between Human Good and Divine Good

If God is not pleased with human good, then what type of good pleases him? The answer is Divine good, which can only be produced in the Power Zone under the control of the Spirit. How do we know this? Christ Himself taught this as He spoke to the disciples about the vine and the branches on the way to the garden at Gethsemane.

John 15:1–2, 4 – I am the true vine ... Every branch in Me [believer in the Security Zone] that does not bear fruit [produces human good outside the Power Zone] He takes away [human good can't be blessed in time or rewarded in eternity]; and every branch that bears fruit [produces Divine good in the Power Zone], He prunes it that it may bear more fruit ... branch cannot bear fruit ... unless it abides in the vine [Power Zone].

Just as the premature fruit that falls off the vine withers and dies, so the believer out of the Power Zone can no longer produce anything that is pleasing to God:

Jn. 15: 5–6 – ... apart from Me you can do nothing. If a man abides not in Me [believer outside the Power Zone] he is thrown away as a branch and withers; and the branches [human good] are thrown into the fire and burned.

The word of God makes it very clear that human good and Divine good have nothing in common. To help you see the difference, let's contrast them in diagram 6.

DIAGRAM 6: The Believer's Production

INSIDE THE POWER ZONE	OUSIDE THE POWER ZONE

DIVINE GOOD

Made Possible by the Cross
Produced Through the Spirit
Blessed in Time
Rewarded in Eternity

HUMAN GOOD

Jn. 15:5 ...Apart from Me You Can Do Nothing
Rom. 8:8 ...Those Who are in the Flesh Cannot Please God
Isa. 64:6 ...Our Righteous Deeds are Like a Filthy Rag

Rejected at the Cross
Produced by Sin Nature
Rejected in Time
Burned in Eternity

Let's back up diagram 6 with scripture references that describe the believer's two categories of production:

1 Cor. 3:11–15 – For no man can lay a foundation other than the one which is laid, which is Jesus Christ. Now if any man builds upon the foundation with gold, silver, precious stones [Divine good], wood, hay, straw [human good], each man's work will become evident; for the day [Judgment Day of Christ—believers only] will show it, because it is to be revealed with fire; and the fire itself will test the quality of each man's work. If any man's work which he has built upon it remains [Divine good], he shall receive a reward [rewards in eternity]. If any man's work is burned up [human good], he shall suffer loss [loss of rewards in eternity], but he himself shall be saved [can't get out of the Security Zone].

It is very important that you fully comprehend this next statement: failure to distinguish between human good and Divine good is one of the major reasons so many Christians are unaware that the Power Zone exists and that it is available simply through confession of sin.

The Bible makes it very clear that human good is produced by the sin nature (flesh) but that Divine good can only be produced through the power of the Spirit, Gal. 5:16–23. The holiness of God cannot bless or reward anything that is produced by our sin nature, which certainly includes self-denial and human good. To help you understand this, let's look at scriptures that contrast Divine good with human good. We need to know what God does with our production, as well as remind ourselves that we can't produce Divine good unless we are inside the Power Zone.

POWER ZONE PRODUCTION: DIVINE GOOD	SIN NATURE PRODUCTION: HUMAN GOOD
I Cor. 3: 12, 14 – gold, silver, precious stones: rewarded	wood, hay, straw: burned
I Cor. 3: 14-15 – work remains: rewards	work burned up: loss of rewards
John 15: 5-6 – branches abiding in Me (Power Zone): bear much fruit	dried up branches: burned
2 Tim. 2: 20-21 – gold and silver vessels: honored, sanctified	wood and earthenware: dishonor
Heb. 6: 7-8 – useful vegetation: blessed	thorns and thistles: burned

These verses should make it very clear just how important the Power Zone is for the believer. Only our production of Divine good inside the Power Zone can be blessed in time and rewarded in eternity. God reveals what awaits the believer who chooses to live, work, and play inside the Power Zone:

2 Cor. 9:8 – And God is able to make all grace abound to you, that always having all sufficiency in everything, you may have an abundance for every good deed.

1 Pet. 1:4 – To obtain an inheritance which is imperishable and undefiled and will not fade away, reserved in heaven for you.

Isaiah 53:11–12 – ... My servant will justify the many, as He will bear their iniquities ... and He will divide the booty with the strong.

In the Isaiah passage, "the booty" obviously refers to eternal rewards, but who are "the strong"? The strong are those believers who chose to live in the Power Zone and thus fulfilled the desire of God expressed in Eph. 3:16–17:

> *... be strengthened with power through His Spirit in the inner man so that Christ may dwell in your hearts ...*

There is no doubt that we can lose rewards in eternity based on our failure to produce Divine good inside the Power Zone during our Christian life.

> *2 John 1:8 – Watch yourselves that you might not lose what we have accomplished, but that you may receive a full reward.*

> *Rev. 3:11 – I am coming quickly; hold fast what you have, in order that no one take your crown.*

And for those believers who choose to walk through life on the dark side, always flirting with one or more of the spiritual death zones, they are still saved, but their rewards (inheritance) in eternity will range from slim to zero:

> *1 Cor. 6:9 – Or do you not know that the unrighteous shall not inherit the kingdom of God?*

Christianity is actually quite simple. We have two choices: live in the Power Zone under the direction of the Spirit, or live in the spiritual death zones under the direction of our sin nature. God deals with us accordingly:

> *Eph. 5:15; Gal. 6:7 – ... be careful how you walk, not as unwise men, but as wise. Do not be deceived, God is not mocked; for whatever a man sows, this he will also reap.*

Heb. 4:13 – And there is no creature hidden from His sight, but all things are naked and open to the eyes of Him to whom we must give account.

Further evidence that human good is unacceptable to God is the revelation that human good plays a major role in sentencing the unbeliever to the lake of fire at the final judgment, Rev. 20:12–13. Because unbelievers rejected Christ as Savior, the only thing they have to stand on is their human good, which will burn in eternity right along with them. The names of unbelievers have been blotted out of the book of life, but their names are in the book of deeds:

Rev. 20:12–15 – And I saw the dead ... standing before the throne, and books were opened ... and the dead were judged from the things written in the books, according to their deeds [human good] ... and death and Hades were thrown into the lake of fire ... And if anyone's name was not found written in the book of life, he was thrown into the lake of fire.

Human good covers any and all commendable-to-the-world works that we produce when we are outside the Power Zone. Just because we are out of fellowship with God does not mean that we are always committing an act of sin. When we are not sinning, it is very likely that we are up to our necks in acts of human good. The tragedy of human good is that much of it could be Divine good if it were produced inside the Power Zone.

God Uses a 100 Percent System

God has a system; His invention of the Power Zone allows our Christian production to be blessed in time and rewarded in eternity. Diagram 7 should help us see what our production choices are in the Christian life.

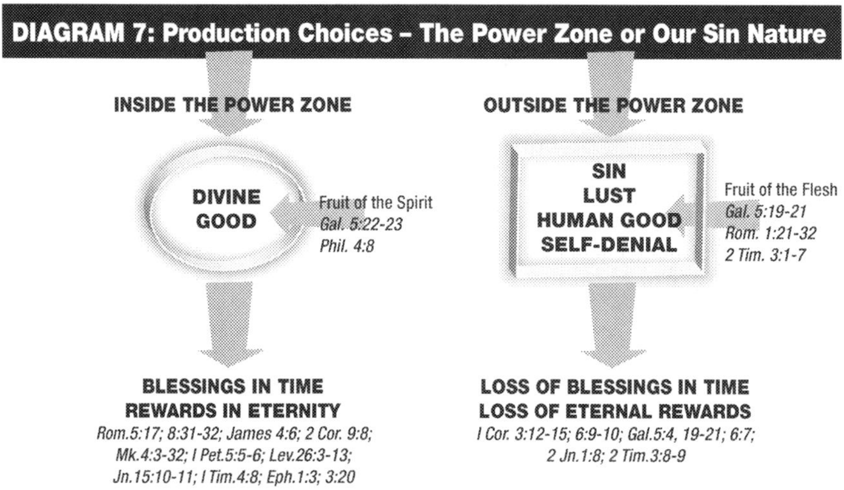

DIAGRAM 7: Production Choices – The Power Zone or Our Sin Nature

INSIDE THE POWER ZONE

OUTSIDE THE POWER ZONE

DIVINE GOOD

Fruit of the Spirit
Gal. 5:22-23
Phil. 4:8

**SIN
LUST
HUMAN GOOD
SELF-DENIAL**

Fruit of the Flesh
Gal. 5:19-21
Rom. 1:21-32
2 Tim. 3:1-7

**BLESSINGS IN TIME
REWARDS IN ETERNITY**
*Rom.5:17; 8:31-32; James 4:6; 2 Cor. 9:8;
Mk.4:3-32; I Pet.5:5-6; Lev.26:3-13;
Jn.15:10-11; I Tim.4:8; Eph.1:3; 3:20*

**LOSS OF BLESSINGS IN TIME
LOSS OF ETERNAL REWARDS**
*I Cor. 3:12-15; 6:9-10; Gal.5:4, 19-21; 6:7;
2 Jn.1:8; 2 Tim.3:8-9*

Basically our two choices are simple: we either produce the fruit of the Spirit or the fruit of the flesh. Keep in mind that the unbeliever can produce a phenomenal amount of human good. However, whatever an unbeliever does is not the Christian way of life. The Christian way of life is executed inside the Power Zone through the power of the Spirit. The believer out of the Power Zone is simply imitating the unbeliever.

The unbeliever can be very moral, very nice, and very sweet and can produce all types of human good. A believer out of fellowship can also do all of those things—when not committing an act of sin. Whether it is produced by the believer out of fellowship or by the unbeliever, God calls human good "filthy rags" in Isa. 64: 6, because it comes from the sin nature and is produced while in the soul status of spiritual death. Remember, God has told us that anything we produce outside the Power Zone, including human good, is not pleasing to Him.

> *Rom. 8:8 – ... those who are carnal cannot please God ...*
> *John 15:5 – ... apart from Me you can do nothing.*

Remember that at any given moment after salvation we are either in the Power Zone or in one of the spiritual death zones. Even if we have just entered the Clone Zone stage of carnality, we are still 100 percent controlled by our sin nature until we return to the Power Zone through the Phone Zone. Even in the Clone Zone, we are never 80 percent spiritual and 20 percent carnal, or any other possible variation of percentages. The Bible is the book of absolutes, and the Spirit-Directed Life is simple: we are either 100 percent in the Power Zone, or we are 100 percent in one of the spiritual death zones. The principle of these two absolute states of soul is stated in Matt. 6: 24:

> *No one can serve two masters; for either he will hate the one and love the other, or he will hold to one and despise the other ...*

Matt. 6: 24 is telling us that the Holy Spirit and our resident sin nature (the flesh) absolutely despise each other; they have nothing in common; they are on opposite ends of the spectrum without any possibility of agreement concerning thought patterns or lifestyles. This post-salvation spiritual warfare continues every moment that we are conscious, from salvation to physical death.

> *Gal. 5:17 – For the flesh sets its desire against the Spirit, and the Spirit against the flesh; for these are in opposition to one another so that you may not do the things that you please.*

Being out of fellowship with God is walking in darkness. Being in fellowship with God is walking in the light. They are as different as night and day, and there are no shades of gray.

> *1 John 1:5–7 – God is light, and in Him [in the Power Zone] is no darkness at all. If we say we have fellowship with Him and walk in darkness [out of the Power Zone due to sin], we lie, and do not practice the truth ... walk in the light [in the Power Zone] ...*

> *Eph. 5:8 – for you were formerly darkness, but now you are light in the Lord; walk as children of light.*

And if you are still in doubt that we can be spiritually dead as believers in Christ, then remember Rom. 8:10:

> *And if Christ is in you, though the body is spiritually*
> *dead because of sin [loss of Spirit empowerment],*
> *yet the Spirit is alive because of righteousness [Spirit*
> *still indwells because God's righteousness was given*
> *to us in the Security Zone].*

In other words, Rom. 8:10 is telling us that while we are temporarily out of the Power Zone due to sin, we are still in the Security Zone. We are temporarily out of fellowship with God when we sin, but we still have a permanent relationship with God because of His grace. Sin causes loss of fellowship and empowerment, not loss of indwelling.

Since human good was first demonstrated by Adam and Eve, let's go back to the Garden for a moment. In the Garden, Satan persuaded Adam and Eve to disobey a loving God and thereby acquire a sin nature, becoming spiritually dead. The first thing spiritually dead Adam and Eve performed was an act of human good: they covered their bodies with fig leaves. The second thing they did was hide from Jesus Christ. Imagine trying to hide from God! It is very important that we understand why they tried to hide—because sin had made them spiritually dead, and they knew it!

Don't you know Satan was immensely proud of himself for deceiving man into becoming spiritually dead? Can't you just see Satan's ego getting pumped in the knowledge that for the rest of human history, humankind would be born spiritually dead, prone to sin and human good? And don't you know Satan was thinking, "I've got you now, God! You'll never get out of this one. If you send me to the lake of fire, you'll have to send the man and woman along with me, because they have just become spiritually dead!"

However, the genius of Satan is no match for the grace of God. Adam and Eve took the grace option of faith alone in Christ alone, just as we have done. God has provided a way for us to be empowered by the Spirit smack dab in the middle of the devil's world. He has done so by the simple, non-meritorious grace procedure of naming our sins directly to Him through the function of our royal priesthood. With a grace provision like that, why waste our time in the Clone Zone?

Tackling the Problem of Sin

Living in the Clone Zone has many more repercussions than just wasting our time. The greatest personal harm comes to us when we live outside the Power Zone. Sin has repercussions that can overflow into all areas of our lives. In order to get a handle on sin, we need to understand exactly what we are dealing with. There are three types of sin, three areas of sin, and three solutions to sin:

DIAGRAM 8: Categorizing Sin

THREE TYPES	THREE AREAS	THREE SOLUTIONS
Mental-Attitude-Sins (Think)	World, Jn. 16:33	Confess, 1 Jn. 1:9
Sins of the Tongue (Say)	Flesh, Gal. 5:16-21	Forget, Phil. 3:13
Overt Sins (Do)	Devil, Eph. 6:12	Grow, Heb. 6:1-2

There are several obvious results of stepping into the Clone Zone through personal sin. The first result is self-induced-misery caused by the mental-attitude sin or sins that caused us to get into the Clone Zone in the first place. Remember that there are three categories of sin: think, say, and do. The sins of say and do are always preceded by the mental-attitude-sins that we think. Some examples of mental-attitude-sins are worry, fear, anxiety, guilt, hatred, jealousy, bitterness, anger, judging, revenge, self-pity, self-righteousness, hypocrisy, selfishness, ingratitude, disrespect, and arrogance. The law of volitional responsibility (suffering the consequences of sin) guarantees that we will have self-induced misery from our mental-attitude-sins.

The second obvious result of stepping into the Clone Zone is Divine discipline. Regardless of what type of sin we are guilty of—

think, say, or do—it is in the Clone Zone that Divine discipline begins. The amount of discipline depends on the severity and frequency of the sin, how it affects others, etc. That's God's sovereign decision, but do not doubt that God disciplines us when we sin.

> *Heb. 12:5 – ... My son, do not regard lightly the discipline of the Lord, nor faint when you are reproved by Him; for those whom the Lord loves He disciplines, and He scourges every son whom He receives.*

The third obvious result of sin is that it often affects others. We carry around with us at all times an attitude, whether good or bad. Even if the sin did not directly affect others, our resultant attitude does. Heb. 12:15 warns us about this:

> *See to it that no one comes short of the grace of God [by failure to confess sin]; that no root of bitterness springing-up causes trouble, and by it many be defiled.*

Sins of the tongue, such as gossip or maligning, can clearly affect others. Gossip is saying something bad about someone that is true, while maligning is saying something bad that is not true. The book of James addresses sins of the tongue in Jm. 3:2–10. For the sake of brevity, let's just look at verses 5–8:

> *Jm. 3:5–8 – So also the tongue is a small part of the body, and yet it boasts of great things. Behold, how great a forest is set aflame by such a small fire! And the tongue is a fire, the very world of iniquity; the tongue is set among our members as that which defiles the entire body, and sets on fire the course of our life, and is set on fire by hell. For every species of beasts and birds, of reptiles and creatures of the sea, is tamed and has been tamed by the human race. But no one can tame the tongue; it is a restless evil and full of deadly poison.*

Needless to say, the tongue can destroy all types of relationships, as well as churches and other large organizations.

Most Christians are very familiar with the overt sins, because they are the ones most emphasized by churches, so there is little need to spend time on them here. However, let's not forget a few things:

- All sin starts with mental-attitude sins.
- If we think something long enough, we will say it.
- If we think it and say it long enough, we are likely to actually do it.

Therefore, it is necessary to keep short accounts with God through confession and spiritual growth:

> *Rom. 12:2 – And do not be conformed to this world, but be transformed by the renewing of your mind, that you may prove what the will of God is, that which is good and acceptable and perfect.*

Concerning the three areas of sin, we all suffer undeservedly at times because of the devil, his world, and the sin natures of other people (flesh). However, most of our suffering is deserved, because we choose to be controlled by our own sin nature instead of by the Spirit. We can live in the Power Zone or in one of the spiritual death zones. The quality of our life is what we make it. We chose it, win or lose it; the world, the flesh, and the devil are never to blame.

Notice in diagram 8 that the solution to personal sin involves three simple steps.

1. The first solution to personal sin is confession. Confession of sin gets us back into the Power Zone, where the Spirit controls our soul.

> *1 Jn. 1:9 – If we confess our sins He is faithful and righteous to forgive us our sins and to cleanse us from all unrighteousness.*

2. The second solution to personal sin is that after we confess it, we forget it. Remember that God forgets sins as soon as we confess them, and He intends that we do the same. He never intends that we develop a guilt complex or dwell on past sins. We won't be in fellowship with God long unless we forget sin and move on.

> *Phil. 3:13–14 – ... one thing I do,: forgetting what lies behind and reaching forward to what lies ahead I press on toward the goal [spiritual maturity] for the prize of the upward call of God in Christ Jesus.*

3. The third solution to personal sin is spiritual growth. Frequency of necessity to confess sin is directly related to spiritual maturity. We'll always need to confess sin, but confession frequency declines with spiritual growth. On a daily basis, spiritual growth should be our number one priority.

> *Heb. 6:1–2 – Therefore leaving the elementary teaching about the Christ, let us press on to maturity, not laying again a foundation of repentance from dead works and of faith toward God, of instruction about washings [baptism], and laying on of hands, and the resurrection of the dead, and eternal judgment.*

Heb. 6:1–2 is telling us outright that it is our responsibility to reach spiritual maturity and that we can't achieve it by repetitive teachings designed for baby believers. It is the responsibility of the pastors of local churches to bring their congregations to spiritual maturity:

> *Eph. 4:8, 11–13 – ... and He [Christ] gave gifts to men ... some as pastors and teachers, for the equipping of the saints for the work of service, to the building up of the body of Christ; until we all attain to the unity of the faith, and of the knowledge of the Son of God, to a mature man, to the measure of the stature which belongs to the fullness of Christ.*

1 Tim. 4:14–16 – Do not neglect the spiritual gift within you ... Take pains with these things; be absorbed in them, so that your progress may be evident to all ... pay close attention to yourself and to your teaching; persevere in these things ...

2 Tim. 2:15 – Study to present yourself approved to God as a workman who does not need to be ashamed, rightly dividing the word of truth.

No congregation can ever grow beyond the spiritual maturity of its pastor. For the pastor, there is no substitute for the hard work of studying and teaching. The congregation cannot apply what it doesn't know.

Spiritual growth is a lengthy process that tests our commitment to have a relationship with God. Regardless of our age and previous lifestyle, God has been waiting to bless our lives in ways we never dreamed possible:

Isa. 30:18 – Therefore the Lord longs to be gracious to you, and therefore He waits on high to have compassion on you ...

Jer. 29:11 – For I know the plans that I have for you, declares the Lord, plans for good and not for evil, to give you hope and a future.

Jer. 33:3 – Call to Me and I will answer you and show you great and mighty things which you do not know.

Rom. 8:32 – He that spared not His own Son but delivered Him up for us all, how shall He not with him freely give us all things?

1 Cor. 2:9 – As it is written, no eye has seen, no ear has heard, no heart can conceive, the things which God has prepared for those who love Him.

Joel 2:25 – Then I will restore to you the years that the swarming locust has eaten ...

The Penalty of Sin versus the Power of Sin

Christians often confuse the penalty of sin with the power of sin. They are not the same thing. For the believer in Christ, the penalty of sin has been permanently canceled, but the power of sin can control us at any given moment from salvation to physical death. Diagram 9 should help explain.

DIAGRAM 9: Distinguishing Between the Penalty and Power of Sin

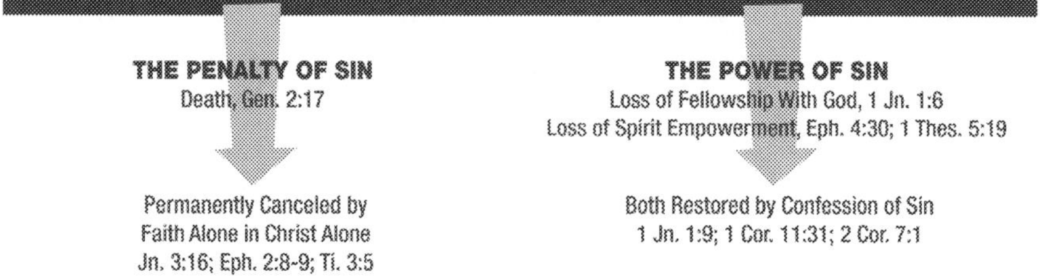

THE PENALTY OF SIN
Death, Gen. 2:17

Permanently Canceled by
Faith Alone in Christ Alone
Jn. 3:16; Eph. 2:8-9; Ti. 3:5

THE POWER OF SIN
Loss of Fellowship With God, 1 Jn. 1:6
Loss of Spirit Empowerment, Eph. 4:30; 1 Thes. 5:19

Both Restored by Confession of Sin
1 Jn. 1:9; 1 Cor. 11:31; 2 Cor. 7:1

The Effect of Sin on the Ministry of the Holy Spirit

Be advised that when we decide to sin and consequently suffer loss of fellowship and empowerment, we have interrupted all the ministries of the Holy Spirit that accompany the Power Zone. Sin makes all ministries of the Spirit nonoperational. They are nonoperational because we are at least grieving and possibly also quenching the Spirit. They are nonoperational because we have chosen sin power over Spirit power as our power source. Although this is never God's will, He allows us to make freewill decisions and suffer the consequences. Besides self-induced misery, Divine discipline, and the adverse effect on others, the consequences of sin include loss of all ministries of the Holy Spirit. Although it may not be all-inclusive, the following list provides examples of Spirit ministries that we lose while we are out of the Power Zone:

1. Teaching and guidance: Jn. 14:16–17, 26; 15:26; 16:13–15; Rom. 8:16; 1 Cor. 2:10–14; 1 Jn. 2:27
2. Sin control: Gal. 5:16; Rom. 8:5a, 6a, 13a
3. Fruits of the Spirit: Gal. 5:22–23; Phil. 4:8
4. Prayer access and inspiration: Ps. 66:18; Isa. 59:2; Jn. 9:31a, 15:7; Eph. 6:18a; Phil. 3:3; Jude 20
5. Intercessory prayer for others: Eph. 6:18b
6. Spiritual gift empowerment: 1 Cor. 12:1, 4–5, 7
7. Soul comforting (peace of mind): Acts 9:31; Jn. 14:26–27
8. Application of the word: Jn. 14:26; Eph. 3:16–20, 5:1–2

While God can and does teach us through Divine discipline, He much prefers to teach us in the Power Zone through His Spirit:

> *Lam. 3:33 – For He does not afflict willingly, or grieve the sons of men.*

Warning Discipline in the Clone Zone

All decisions to sin have consequences, even if we're in the first stage of spiritual death, the Clone Zone. Let's review some verses in Romans reminding us that sin causes spiritual death:

> *Rom. 8:6a, 8, 13a – For the mind set on the flesh is death ... and those who are in the flesh cannot please God ... for if you are living according to the flesh, you must die [spiritually].*

One of the greatest dangers of stepping into the Clone Zone is that we may decide to perpetuate our spiritual death status by failing to confess sins. Besides the negative consequences of self-induced misery, an adverse effect on others, and loss of all ministries of the Holy Spirit, God's warning discipline begins in the Clone

Zone. Warning discipline is simply God warning us to take the grace option and confess sin.

> *Rev. 3:19–20 – As many as I love, I rebuke [warning discipline] and punish. Therefore be eager and repent. Behold, I stand at the door and knock [warning discipline]. If anyone hears My voice and opens the door [confesses sins], I will come in to him and dine with him, and he with Me [back in the Power Zone, fellowship, and empowerment restored].*

> *James 5:9 – Do not complain, believers, against one another, that you yourselves may not be judged; behold, the Judge is standing right at the door [warning discipline].*

> *Job 5:18 – For He inflicts pain [warning discipline], and gives relief [when we confess].*

> *1 Cor. 11:30a – For this reason [believers partaking of the communion elements while out of fellowship] many are weak [warning discipline] ...*

God warns us that if we fail to confess sin in the Clone Zone, self-induced misery and Divine discipline will intensify in the Groan and Stone Zones, because Divine discipline is directly proportional to our level of spiritual degeneracy.

> *Pss. 7:12 – If a man does not repent, He will sharpen His sword; He has bent His bow and made it ready. He has also prepared for Himself deadly weapons; He makes His arrows fiery shafts.*

> *Pss. 7:15–16a – He dug a grave [spiritually dead believer in the Clone Zone] and hollowed it out [failure to confess, leading into the Groan Zone], and has fallen into the hole which he made [dying*

discipline in the Stone Zone]. His frustration shall return on his own head [self-induced misery].

It is important to remember that in addition to sin, our sin nature produces human good and self-denial, which are also very displeasing to God. In Galatians chapter 5, Paul warns the Galatians that Divine discipline also applies to the religious believer who is counterfeiting spirituality through human good and self-denial.

Gal. 5:4 – You have been cut off from Christ, you who are seeking to be justified by law [religious do-good-ism]; you have drifted off course from grace.

Why are the religious do-gooders subject to Divine discipline? Through their colossal, self-righteous arrogance, they have substituted their sin-nature production of human good and self-denial for the power of the Holy Spirit. They prefer human do-good-ism to living in the Power Zone. They have become like the scribes and Pharisees:

Matt. 23:29 – Woe to you, scribes and Pharisees, hypocrites! For you are like whitewashed tombs which on the outside appear beautiful, but inside they are full of dead men's bones and all uncleanness.

Lest we end this chapter on a negative note, remember that in any of the spiritual death zones except the Bone Zone, we still have the grace option of returning to the Power Zone through confession of sin:

Heb. 4:15–16 – For we do not have a high priest who cannot sympathize with our weaknesses, but one who has been tempted in all things as we are, yet without sin [Jesus Christ]. Let us therefore draw near with confidence to the throne of grace, that we may receive mercy and may find grace to help in time of need [God's faithfulness in forgiving our sins upon confession].

And let's not forget that even when we do sin, the grace of God provides us with a defense attorney who never has lost and never will lose a case:

1 Jn. 2:1 – ... And if anyone sins, we have an Advocate [defense attorney] with the Father, Jesus Christ the righteous.

Since Jesus Christ lived in the Power Zone during His earthly ministry and then left it for us so that we could imitate Him, Eph. 5:1, it goes without saying that we should be living in the Power Zone just as He did:

1 Jn. 2:6 – The one who says he abides in Him ought himself to walk in the same manner as He walked.

Just because we should live in the Power Zone as Christ did doesn't mean that we will. In this chapter we have seen the Divine discipline that awaits us in the Clone Zone. In Chapter 7, "Spiritual Death Roulette," we will take a brief look at what awaits us when we decide to perpetuate our pathetic pursuits and raunchy relationships into the other zones of spiritual death.

CHAPTER 6 KEY POINTS

- Any act of sin means that we have cloned ourselves under the only power we knew as unbelievers—our old sin nature. (p. 113)
- Being in the Clone Zone means being in the first zone of spiritual death. (p. 118)
- Human good consists of the so-called "good deeds" that we produce while we are out of fellowship with God. (p. 122-123)
- Spirituality is living inside the Power Zone, in fellowship with God, receiving power, motivation, and direction from the Holy Spirit. (p. 124)
- Satan's two-pronged attack consists of cosmic chaos (sin and lust) and counterfeit spirituality (human good and self-denial). (p. 126)
- We are never 80 percent spiritual and 20 percent carnal or any other possible variation of percentages. We are either 100 percent in the Power Zone or 100 percent in one of the spiritual death zones. (p. 133)

CHAPTER 7: SPIRITUAL DEATH ROULETTE

Satan Exploits Our Bad Decisions

There is nothing Satan likes better than the believer out of fellowship with God who has decided to stay and play in his world. We enter the devil's world through sin, and we stay and play when we decide not to confess sin and then follow it with spiritual growth. Even after confession, failure to grow spiritually means we will soon be right back in the devil's world.

When we are in one of the spiritual death zones, Satan is like a cat torturing a little mouse before eating it, but with one significant difference: Satan will prolong our misery for years, if possible, by enticing us into the retrogressive zones of moral or immoral degeneracy. It doesn't matter whether we are trying to satisfy our lusts through immoral degeneracy or trying to counterfeit spirituality through moral degeneracy—in other words, human good and self-denial. Either way, Satan and his army of demons rejoice when our bad decisions force God to intensify His discipline. The purpose of God's discipline is always to persuade us to return to the Power Zone, where we can be under the protective umbrella of His loving grace. Although God disciplines us in grace, we never recognize grace when we are up to our necks in self-induced misery and divine discipline.

Praising the Remnant

Before we discuss the progressive divine discipline that awaits believers who choose to live their lives rejecting God's word, let's take a moment to praise the believers who generally only move back and forth between the Power Zone and the Clone Zone, and only rarely stray into the other spiritual death zones. Both humanly and spiritually speaking, these believers are the salt-of-the-earth types who make the greatest friends, spouses, parents, neighbors, soldiers, and citizens. They have decided to follow Christ, live the moral life, observe the law, and be an example to their families, their churches, and their fellow citizens. In short, they bless others by association. With regard to spiritual growth, they may be babies, adolescents, or mature, but whatever their status, they are consistently growing. When God decides to call these believers home, they die under the concept of dying grace, which is exactly the opposite of the sin unto death. God may take them instantly or over a prolonged period; their death may be painless or painful, but what is striking is their trust in God and their application of His word in life or in death.

My late wife, Sharon, the most precious little morsel of feminine pulchritude I've known so far in my lifetime, was promoted to heaven under dying grace. She was a perfect illustration of the word "remnant". She was Tinkerbell come to life, all 4'11" of her and 100 pounds soaking wet. While she was in the process of dying from liver cancer, with her perfect little body swollen up like a basketball, she would sit on the edge of the bed in ICU. Unable to speak because of the tubes down her throat, she would look me in the eye, smile, hum a tune, and swing her swollen legs and feet in time to her self-made music. That was her way of telling me that she was okay with the situation and that I was to be okay with it too. I pray I will be that courageous in death. I have missed her more than words can express.

This category of Christ follower like Sharon is called the remnant because they are Christ followers moment by moment, day by day, and year by year. Collectively, the remnant is the backbone of any priest nation such as the United States. A priest nation stands or falls on the basis of the size and influence of its remnant. When a priest nation falls, it falls for spiritual reasons: Isaiah 5: 13; Hosea 4: 1-6; Mat. 21: 43

Obviously, believers in the remnant cannot be classified with the believers we are about to study who receive progressive Divine discipline because they habituate the Groan and Stone Zones. Believers who live in these zones live there because they have temporarily, or perhaps permanently, turned their backs on Christianity to pursue their lusts, to follow false doctrine, and to generally live a life of sin outside the Power Zone. It is their conscious, consistent, and willing decisions to do so that keep them in their downhill race to self-destruction.

The grace solution to sin is simple, and by now you should be very familiar with it. We get back into the Power Zone through the Phone Zone, confession of sin, and we avoid letting sin rule our lives through spiritual growth. An interesting question arises. Why don't we just keep things simple by confessing sin immediately in the Clone Zone, then grow spiritually daily and avoid venturing into the Groan and Stone Zones? The answer is partly because sin is so attractive, partly because our arrogance is so powerful, and partly because Satan knows exactly what or whom to dangle in front of us to keep us entangled within our areas of weakness. We are warned not to get tangled up in areas where we are prone to sin:

> *Heb. 12:1 – ... let us lay aside every weight, and the sin which so easily entangles us, and let us run with endurance the race that is set before us*

How does Satan know our areas of weakness? He has a massive and highly organized army of demons, with at least one assigned to every believer who is advancing spiritually. Depending upon our effectiveness against the devil's world, demons are assigned to us accordingly.

> *Eph. 6:12 – ... For our struggle is ... against the rulers [archon = demon generals], against the powers [exousias = demon officers], against the world forces of this darkness [kosmokrators = elite*

> *demon operatives], against the spirits of evil in the
> heavenlies. [pneumatikos = rank-and-file demons]*

Eph. 6:12 lists Satan's demons in order of rank. Our effectiveness as Christians dictates which rank of demons is assigned to us. However, if our lifestyle involves living in one of the spiritual death zones, Satan doesn't need to sic a demon on us, because we are our own worst enemy. We can mess things up quite well on our own, thank you, and Satan will spend his time trying to sidetrack the more effective believers while we surround ourselves with people of similar sin-trends. Be advised that we'll remain in spiritual trouble until we change lifestyles and friends.

In addition to attacking individual believers, Satan attacks the population of entire nations through the "isms" of this world. Some of these include the following:

- Socialism – designed to destroy the national economy and the middle class
- Globalism – designed to destroy national sovereignty and border integrity
- Multiculturalism – designed to destroy a nation's common cultural heritage and therefore national patriotism

Try winning a war without patriots! One major reason America's state, local, and national governments have run amuck with promoters of these types of evil is because in any nation, spiritual morons always outnumber and therefore outvote the spiritually informed. That is the precise reason our Bible scholar Founding Fathers deliberately designed a Republic with a limited voting franchise instead of a Democracy with an unlimited voting franchise. There are no Divine institutions that spiritual morons can't destroy.

For our own protection, God has assigned to every believer at least one guardian angel to protect us from our own stupidity and from the devil's world:

Psalms 91:11 – For He will give His angels charge concerning you, to guard you in all your ways.

Why We Need to Keep Short Accounts with God

Since so many of us are so hardheaded about sin, we should learn exactly what awaits us when we venture into the progressive Divine discipline of the Clone, Groan, and Stone Zones. Diagram 1 reveals the progressive stages of Divine discipline.

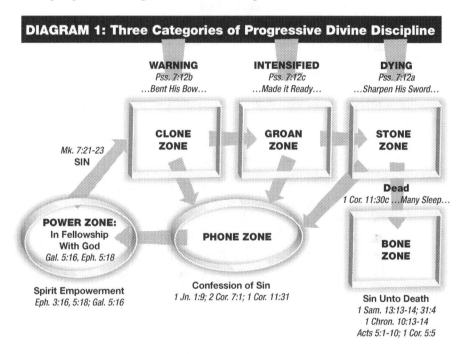

DIAGRAM 1: Three Categories of Progressive Divine Discipline

WARNING	INTENSIFIED	DYING
Pss. 7:12b	*Pss. 7:12c*	*Pss. 7:12a*
...Bent His Bow...	*...Made it Ready...*	*...Sharpen His Sword...*

Mk. 7:21-23
SIN

CLONE ZONE — GROAN ZONE — STONE ZONE

Dead
1 Cor. 11:30c *...Many Sleep...*

POWER ZONE:
In Fellowship
With God
Gal. 5:16, Eph. 5:18

PHONE ZONE

BONE ZONE

Spirit Empowerment
Eph. 3:16, 5:18; Gal. 5:16

Confession of Sin
1 Jn. 1:9; 2 Cor. 7:1; 1 Cor. 11:31

Sin Unto Death
1 Sam. 13:13-14; 31:4
1 Chron. 10:13-14
Acts 5:1-10; 1 Cor. 5:5

It is important to understand the concept of time when looking at diagram 1. We get out of the Power Zone and into the Clone Zone immediately when we commit sin because we have just grieved the Holy Spirit, Eph. 4:30. We enter the Groan Zone at the moment we decide we are going to remain in our sins instead of confessing them, because at that point we have taken sin to the next step and quenched the Spirit, 1 Thes. 5:19. The transition period between the Clone Zone and Groan Zone can therefore be extremely short.

On the other hand, the transition period between the Groan Zone and Stone Zone could be months or even years, depending on lifestyle and how fast scar tissue is being accumulated. Any type of addiction will accelerate the process. When hardness of the heart causes absolute negativity toward the word of God in the Stone Zone, God has the option of taking us out quickly or prolonging our discipline and self-induced misery. Once believers enter the Stone Zone, only God knows for sure if they will ever recover. Usually the best we can do for the Stone Zone believer is to give them Divine viewpoint (the word of God) and pray for them. To understand what Divine discipline is like in the Groan and Stone Zones, read what David had to say about God's discipline to him over Operation Bathsheba in Psalms 38 and Psalms 51:1–17.

The transition period between the Groan Zone and Bone Zone varies widely in number of years because developing scar tissue and hardness of the heart takes time. The transition period between the Stone Zone and Bone Zone depends entirely on the type and duration of dying discipline that God decides to administer.

The transition between the Stone and Bone Zone is obvious, simply because if we're in the Bone Zone, we are physically dead and thus face to face with Jesus Christ. Overall, moving from the Clone Zone all the way into the Bone Zone can take many years. During those years, there are likely to be so many variables that only God knows precisely where the believer is. Spiritual death zone roulette, anyone?

We will examine the last three zones in this one combined chapter to avoid dwelling too long on the negative. It is important to understand that while self-induced misery and Divine discipline begin in the Clone Zone, they are progressively intensified throughout the Groan and Stone Zones. In addition to self-induced misery and Divine discipline, we have to add scar tissue of the soul. Scar tissue is caused by consistent rejection of God's word and other sins, including mental-attitude-sins, fornication, promiscuity, and adultery.

> *Eph. 4:17–18 – ... walk no longer as the Gentiles walk [unbelievers], in the futility of their mind [rejecting God's word], being darkened in their understanding [scar tissue], excluded from the life of God [out of the Power Zone] because of the ignorance that is in them, because of the hardness of their heart [Stone Zone].*

Scar tissue not only alienates us from God, it destroys capacity for love and divorces us from reality. Scar tissue begins in the Groan Zone, intensifies in the Stone Zone, and completely covers our soul just prior to God placing us under the sin unto death. The sin unto death is not a single sin, but rather a lifestyle of sin in which we reach the point of no return.

You will notice at the top of diagram 1 that God adjusts His discipline according to which zone of spiritual death we are in. We get warning discipline in the Clone Zone, intensified discipline in the Groan Zone, and dying discipline in the Stone Zone. Finally, we are removed by the sin unto death in the Bone Zone. As Psalms 7:12 shows, God bends His bow when we enter the Clone Zone, He makes it ready when we enter the Groan Zone, and He sharpens His sword when we're in the Stone Zone. "Sharpening His sword" is an idiom for impending capital punishment.

God's discipline adjusts to our self-destructive decisions as we retrogress into the three spiritual death zones. Psalms 7:15 is a great illustration of our stages of spiritual self-destruction

> *He has dug a pit [Clone Zone] and hollowed it out [Groan Zone], and has fallen into the hole [Stone Zone].*

We dig a pit in the Clone Zone when we decide to sin. Self-induced misery and warning discipline begins.

When we refuse to confess sins, we enter the Groan Zone, digging deeper and wider into the pit and becoming totally preoccupied with our sins. The frantic search for happiness begins. Scar tissue of the soul begins to form, while self-induced misery and Divine discipline intensifies.

If we still refuse to confess sins, we enter the Stone Zone and start to bury ourselves in the pit with a lifestyle of sin. Hardness of the heart begins, and the frantic search for happiness intensifies, while scar tissue, self-induced misery, and Divine discipline are all maximized.

The main thing to understand about the spiritual death zones is that only misery awaits us, because self-induced misery, Divine discipline, and scar tissue are all progressive. When we are in the final stages of the Stone Zone, God may keep us alive for an indefinite amount of time to test other believers or to serve as an example of how a spiritual loser lives. Though physically alive, we are a spiritually dead man walking. But as diagram 1 illustrates, let us never forget that until God actually takes our soul and spirit to be with Him, we still have the option of returning to the Power Zone:

> *Heb. 4:15–16 – For we do not have a high priest [Jesus Christ] who cannot sympathize with our weaknesses, but one who has been tempted in all things as we are, yet without sin. Let us therefore draw near with confidence to the throne of grace that we may receive mercy and may find grace to help in time of need.*

We saw in the last chapter the Divine discipline that awaits us in the Clone Zone. It is the smart believer who keeps short accounts with God by confessing sin immediately in the Clone Zone and not going beyond grieving the Holy Spirit.

Entering the Groan Zone: The Frantic Search for Happiness

We leave the Power Zone and enter the Clone Zone through personal sin, at which point we are grieving the Spirit. We make matters worse by quenching the Spirit when we make a decision to remain out of fellowship with God and stay under the power of our sin nature. At this point, because He is now quenched, the Holy Spirit is going to start banging on the door of our soul instead of just knocking.

Rev. 3:19b – ... be eager therefore, and repent.

To repent means to change your mind about your direction in life. God warns us to change through His word and through the power of the Spirit. The Spirit will find a way to warn us that we are not in a good place and to return to the Power Zone. When we fail to open the door through confession of sin, Rev. 3:20, we have just quenched the Holy Spirit and entered the Groan Zone.

It is the unwise believer who refuses to heed the warnings of the Holy Spirit. We do that when we decide, for whatever reason, that we are not going to confess our sins. The reason makes no difference, including our spiritual ignorance that confession of sin is necessary in order to recover fellowship with God. God holds us equally responsible for sins of omission as well as sins of commission. Perhaps we missed a Bible class when 1 John 1:9 was being taught.

When we make the decision to continue in our sins from the Clone Zone, we have moved into the Groan Zone, and we are further alienated from God. It is important to understand that we are not more out of fellowship with God in the Groan Zone, because we were already 100 percent out of fellowship in the Clone Zone. However, we are further alienated from God in the Groan Zone because we are building scar tissue on our soul and therefore are much less likely to confess sin and return to the Power Zone.

Deciding to remain in our sins mean that we build up defense mechanisms against God, such as refusing to take in His word and grow spiritually. This causes our sin-trends to morph into habit, because it stimulates our lust patterns, especially if we are sinning in our areas of weakness. As our lust patterns stimulate our emotions, we are fooled into believing that stimulation is happiness. That's when the futile, frantic search for happiness begins. Solomon makes this clear in Ecclesiastes and Proverbs. At that point, we can kiss the inner peace of true happiness good-bye until we decide to return to the Power Zone.

Returning to the Power Zone becomes progressively more difficult as we log time in the spiritual death zones. The longer we stay out of fellowship with God, the less likely we are to confess sins. The result is that we perpetuate our soul status of spiritual death, alienated from God, and God begins to intensify our Divine discipline. Once we add to the Divine discipline our self-induced misery and our scar tissue, we've really got some serious spiritual problems. The longer we refuse to confess sins and grow spiritually, the bigger our spiritual problems become. Why do we have to confess and grow spiritually? Because confession alone does not remove scar tissue; only spiritual growth removes scar tissue from the soul.

Entering the Stone Zone: Flirting with Dying Discipline

As previously stated, it would be very difficult to say at exactly what point we leave the Groan Zone and enter the Stone Zone, but it happens because we consistently reject the word of God and continue in our sins. This soul status is best described in Romans 1:21–32.

As we have seen, what makes the Groan Zone so dangerous is that scar tissue of the soul begins here. When the Bible speaks of a heart being "darkened," it usually refers to scar tissue:

> *Rom. 1:21 – For even though they knew God, they did not honor Him as God, or give thanks; but they became futile in their speculations, and their foolish heart was darkened.*

What makes the Stone Zone so dangerous is that hardness of the heart begins here:

> *Eph. 4: 18 – being darkened in their understanding, excluded from the life of God [the Power Zone],*

because of the ignorance that is in them, because of the hardness of their heart;

Rom. 1: 21, 24, 26, 28, 32 – For even though they knew God, they did not honor Him as God ... therefore God gave them over in the lusts of their hearts to impurity ... gave them over to degrading passions ... gave them over to a depraved mind ... and although they know the ordinance of God that those who practice such things are worthy of death, they not only do the same, but also give hearty approval to those who practice them.

The repeated phrase "God gave them over" simply means that God has given them numerous opportunities, most likely over a period of years, to change their lifestyle, friends, bad habits, addictions, etc., but they have constantly said no to fellowship with God, no to recovery, and yes to their lifestyle of sin. Not only do they remain in their lifestyle, they recruit others and encourage participation in their self-destructive ways. Birds of a feather degenerate together.

In addition to the Romans verses, Paul gives another great description of the Stone Zone believers in Ephesians:

Eph. 4:19 – and they, being past feeling, have given themselves over to sensuality, to work all uncleanness with greediness.

God provides advance warning of exactly what lies ahead for the non-repentant Stone Zone believer:

Rev. 3:15–16 – I know your deeds, that you are neither cold [unbelievers] nor hot [mature believers] ... so because you are lukewarm [always negative to God's word], I will vomit you out of My mouth [sin unto death].

This passage tells us that when we have been consistently negative to God's word, have acquired maximum scar tissue and hardness of the heart, and have ignored all His Divine discipline designed to bring us back into the Power Zone, the only thing left for us is removal through the sin unto death. The time and method of death is God's sovereign decision.

Despite deceiving outward appearances and in some cases financial prosperity, the Stone Zone believers are miserable Christians who do not understand why they are miserable. As potential inductees into the Bone Zone, they are described by the Apostle John in Rev. 3:17:

> *Because you say "I am rich, and have become wealthy, and have need of nothing," you don't know that you are wretched [stressed out], and miserable [limited enjoyment of possessions] and poor [in spiritual poverty] and blind [can't see reality] and naked [defenseless against the devil's world].*

We are commanded to encourage Stone Zone believers out of their lifestyle of sin before it is too late:

> *Heb. 3:13 – But encourage one another ... as long as it is still called "Today," lest any one of you be hardened by the deceitfulness of sin.*

A Panoramic View of Progressive Divine Discipline

Perhaps the best way to view the stages of Divine discipline is through a comparison of verses illustrating the progression of self-induced misery, discipline, scar tissue, and hardness of the heart. The verses used in the comparison are just examples and by no means a complete reference. Numerous other passages of scripture would also apply. In diagram 2, I have arranged the verses to show progression from left to right on the same line across the spiritual death zones:

DIAGRAM 2: Progressive Divine Discipline Across Spiritual Death Zones

CLONE ZONE	GROAN ZONE	STONE ZONE
Warning Discipline Self-induce Misery and Divine Discipline Begins	**Intensified Discipline** Scar Tissue of the Soul Begins Self-Induced Misery and Divine Discipline Intensifies	**Dying Discipline** Hardness of the Heart Begins Scar Tissue Increases Self-Induced Misery and Divine Discipline Maximized
1 Cor. 11:30 – Many are Weak	*– Many are Sick*	*Pss. 38:17 – Ready to Fall*
Pss. 38:6 – I Mourn All Day	*v8 – Heart Agitation…I Groan*	*v17 – Continuous Sorrow*
Pss. 38:2 – Your Hand Pressed Down on Me	*v9 – My Groaning Not Hidden*	*v2 – Your Arrows Sunk Deep*
James 5:9 – The Judge is Standing at the Door	*Mat. 7:2 – Judgment Measured Back to You*	*Pss. 7:13 – He has Prepared Deadly Weapons…Fiery Shafts*
Job 5:18 – Bruised	*– Wounded*	*Heb. 12:6 – Skinned Alive*
Gal. 5:4 – Drifted Off Course	*2 Thes. 2:11 – Under Strong Delusion*	*Pss. 7:14 – In Pain with Wickedness*
Heb. 12:5 – Whom the Lord Loves He Disciplines	*Pss. 6:6 – My Bed Swims with Tears …Eyes Wasted with Grief*	*Pss. 38:7, 10 – No Soundness in My Flesh …Strength Fails*
Pss. 7:16 – Frustration Returns on Your Own Head	*Eph. 4:18 – Heart Darkened*	*Eph. 4:18; Heb. 3:13 – Heart Hardened by Sin*
Rev. 3:20 – Behold, I Stand at the Door and Knock	*James 4:4 – Friend of the World, Enemy of God*	*1 Jn. 3:8, 10 – Agents/Discpiles of the Devil*
Pss. 7:16 – Your Mischief Returns on Your Own Head	*Rom. 8:7 – Hostile Toward God*	*Jn. 15:23 – Haters of God*
Rev. 3:19a – Those Whom I Love, I Rebuke	*Heb. 4:7 – Do Not Harden Your Hearts*	*Rom. 1:28 – Given Over to a Depraved Mind*
Rev. 3:19b – Those Whom I Love, I Discipline	*Titus 1:16 – Deny God, Disobedient, Can't Produce*	*2 Tim. 3:9 – They Will Not Make Further Progress*
		Rev. 3:16 – I Will Vomit You Out of My Mouth

You will notice that the Bone Zone is not included in diagram 2 because the Bone Zone believer has been removed by God through the sin unto death. For scripture references, see diagram 1.

The Purpose behind God's Discipline

Diagram 2 should make it clear that God is not going to just sit back and let us self-destruct without taking corrective measures. However, let us never forget even for a moment that God disciplines us in grace through His love.

> *Heb. 12:10 – For they [our fathers] disciplined us for a short time as seemed best to them, but He disciplines us for our good, that we may share His holiness [living in the Power Zone].*

If you have ever disciplined a child in your infinite love for that child, you should have some idea about the concept of Divine discipline. God loves us with a capacity for love we can't fully comprehend. He wants only the very best for us, which is why He sent the very best——His uniquely born Son—that we might have life and have it more abundantly, Jn. 10:10. It is because He wants us to live the abundant life that He not only disciplines us, but also intensifies the discipline progressively across the spiritual death zones.

Some of us are very hardheaded when it comes to sin. For those who are, be assured that God knows better than Satan ever could how to discipline us in a manner that will get our attention. Satan comes after us in hatred, but God comes after us in love, as a parent searching for a lost child. Satan laughs *at us* when we are in a spiritual death zone, but God laughs *with us* when we return to the Power Zone. Although we may be in great anguish of soul and even in physical pain because of Divine discipline, He punishes us because of His love.

> *Lam. 3:32–33 – For if He causes grief, then He will have compassion according to His loving kindness, for He does not afflict willingly ...*

Regardless of which spiritual death zone we are in, the sooner we get back into the Power Zone, the greater the blessings that await us. Only God can turn discipline into blessing and adversity into prosperity.

> *Rom. 8:28 – For we know that God causes all things to work together for good to those who love God, to those who are called according to His purpose.*

The only way we can fulfill God's purpose for our lives is by exploiting His grace. We will examine this issue in Chapter 8, "Exploiting Grace in the Power Zone."

CHAPTER 7 KEY POINTS

- Satan and his army of demons rejoice when our decisions to remain out of the Power Zone force God to intensify His discipline. (p. 147)
- The remnant: Salt-of-the-earth believers who only rarely stray any farther than the Clone Zone. (p. 148)
- The smart believer confesses sins immediately in the Clone Zone and avoids venturing into the Groan and Stone Zones. (p. 149)
- Satan always knows our areas of weakness. (p. 149)
- The progressive stages of Divine discipline are: Warning (Clone Zone); Intensified (Groan Zone); Dying (Stone Zone). (p. 151, diagram 1)
- Self-induced misery begins in the Clone Zone. The frantic search for happiness and scar tissue begins in the Groan Zone. Hardness of the heart begins in the Stone Zone. (p. 152-156)
- Birds of a feather degenerate together. (p. 157)
- Divine discipline is progressive across the spiritual death zones. (p. 159)
- The purpose behind progressive Divine discipline is to get us back inside the Power Zone. (p. 160)

CHAPTER 8: EXPLOITING GRACE
IN THE POWER ZONE

The Church Age and the Power Zone

Within the context of this book, I have mentioned the term Church Age numerous times. This term is important for two reasons. First, because it is the current dispensation—which I will explain in a moment—and second, because it carries many unprecedented privileges for Christ followers that function only inside the Power Zone. Dispensations are divisions of human history designed by God in eternity past to facilitate the progressive revelation of His comprehensive plan, which is revealed from Genesis to Revelation. Every dispensation has a beginning point and an ending point. For example, the Church Age began on the Day of Pentecost, Acts 2: 1, and it will end with the Rapture of the Church, 1 Thes. 4:16–17.

Jesus Christ Himself told the eleven Apostles (minus Paul), in Acts 1:7, that God the Father had designed dispensations:

> He said to them, "It is not for you to know the times [chronos – lengths] or seasons [kairos – characteristics] which the Father has fixed by His own authority."

The only reason it wasn't for the eleven Apostles to know the times or seasons is because the mystery doctrines about the Church Age would be revealed only to the twelfth Apostle, Paul, who would then give that information to the other Apostles and the churches.

> Eph. 3:1–2, 5, 8–9 – For this reason I, Paul, the prisoner of Christ Jesus for the sake of you Gentiles, if indeed you have heard of the stewardship [oikonomia – dispensation] of God's grace [Church Age] which

was given to me for you ... which in other generations was not made known to the sons of men, as it has now been revealed to His holy Apostles and prophets in the Spirit; To me ... this grace was given ... to bring to light what is the administration [oikonomia] of the mystery [the Church Age and its body of doctrines] which for all ages has been hidden in God ...

While there may be disagreement among men over how to divide the dispensations, Heb. 11:3 makes it clear that the dispensations are ordained by God from eternity past:

By faith we understand that the worlds [Gr. aion = ages or dispensations] were prepared by the word of God, so that what is being seen [the unfolding of history] has not come to pass from those who are visible [dispensations are not of man's invention].

There are four Greek words used for dispensations in the Bible: *Chronos*, time in length or sequence of events, 1 Thes. 5:1; *Kairos*, characteristics of an era, Rom. 5:6; *Oikonomia*, used by Paul for the Church Age, Eph. 3:2,5, 8–9; and *Aion*, a category of human history, Heb. 11:3. The New Testament uses words or phrases such as "administration," "stewardship," "worlds," "ages," "times," "seasons," and "the fellowship of the mystery" to describe dispensations or portions of dispensations.

What does understanding dispensations have to do with exploiting grace in the Power Zone? Simply this: the Power Zone was never available to believers until the Church Age dispensation, because Christ had not yet demonstrated its power. After He was resurrected, ascended, and was glorified at the right hand of the Father, the gift of the Spirit was near.

John 7:39 – ... the Spirit was not yet given, because Jesus was not yet glorified.

Acts 1:5 – ... you shall be baptized with the Spirit not many days from now.

Recognizing Spiritual Royalty

As believers in the Church Age, we have Divine operating assets never available to believers in Old Testament dispensations. For example, with the one-time event of the Baptism of the Holy Spirit at the moment of salvation, we were placed into permanent union with Christ in the Security Zone. How do we know the Baptism of the Spirit is a one-time event? The aorist tense of "were all baptized" in 1 Cor. 12:13 means a single event that occurred in one point of time with results that continue forever. The Baptism of the Spirit occurs once, has nothing to do with water, and cannot be improved upon. Water baptism has never saved anyone. It is faith alone in Christ alone that saves us and prompts the Spirit to place us into permanent union with Christ in the Security Zone. Only Church Age believers are in union with Christ. We are spiritual royalty!

As spiritual royalty, we are the body of Christ during the Church Age, 1 Cor. 12:27, and the bride of Christ for all eternity, Rev. 19:7. Because we are spiritual royalty, we have the universal indwelling and empowering of the Holy Spirit. Since we are permanently "in Christ" in the top circle (Security Zone), we are permanently indwelled by the Spirit, Jn. 14:17. Because we are permanently indwelled by the Spirit, we have the option of being empowered by the Spirit in the bottom circle, the Power Zone, Eph. 5:18. In addition, all ministries of the Holy Spirit become operational to us inside the Power Zone. But God still isn't through giving to us. We have the mind of Christ in the completed Bible, 1 Cor. 2:16. We have all the mystery doctrines of the Church Age revealed to us in the New Testament, Eph. 3:8–10. We have at least one spiritual gift, Rom. 12:6. We have a better covenant with better promises, Heb. 8:6. And we have the universal priesthood of the believer, 1 Pet. 2:5, 9, Rev. 1:6, 5:10. The universal priesthood means that all of us are in full-time Christian service, regardless of our spiritual gift. As priests ourselves, we have the privilege of approaching the throne of grace directly, without going through an intermediary.

> *Heb. 7:12 – For when the priesthood is changed, of necessity there takes place a change of law also.*

There is no doubt about it: as Church Age believers, we are a new creature upon the earth.

> *2 Cor. 5:17 – Therefore if any one is in Christ [Security Zone], he is a new creature.*

However, Jesus Christ, in His "Parable of the Sower," makes it clear that not all believers will exploit grace in the Power Zone.

The Parable of the Sower

In His Parable of the Sower in Luke chapter 8, Jesus Christ tells us that there are three types of new creatures (believers) in the Church Age.

DIAGRAM 1: Parable of the Sower – Luke 8:4-15

SOWER = Any Believer Giving the Gospel or Communicating God's Word
SEED = The Gospel or the Doctrine Being Communicated

THREE CATEGORIES OF BELIEVERS IN THE CHURCH AGE

Accept Gospel, Reject Growth *Verses 6 & 13*	**Partial Growth, Get Distracted** *Verses 7 & 14*	**Persistent Growth** *Verses 8 & 15; Mat. 13:23*
"Spin-Off" After Salvation	"Spin-Off" After Limited Growth	Grow from Salvation on… (Baby, Adolescent, Mature)
Saved No Blessings No Rewards	Saved Limited Blessings Limited Rewards	Saved Many Blessings Many Rewards

---

The challenge for us is to stand fast in the last column in order to have a strong relationship with God, enjoy many blessings during our lifetime, and receive many rewards for all eternity.

1 Cor. 16:13 – Watch, stand fast in the faith, be brave, be strong.

2 Cor. 9:8, 5:10 – And God is able to make all grace abound to you, that always having all sufficiency in everything, you may have an abundance for every good deed [Divine good]. For we must all appear before the judgment seat of Christ, that each one may be recompensed for his deeds in the body ... whether good or bad.

The Parable of the Sower has national, personal, and eternal implications. It is obvious in our founding documents that the United States is a priest nation to God. It is impossible for God not to bless this nation when the remnant of believers in column three is large enough. Conversely, it is impossible for God not to discipline this nation when the remnant is too small.

National Implications: The United States is a priest nation, and every believer is a priest.

In the Church Age, Christ transfers priest nation status from Jews to Gentiles, the Christian Church replaces Israel, and every believer is a priest, replacing the specialized priesthood, Mat. 21:43; Luke 21:24; Acts 13:46; Rom. 11:17, 25; 1 Pet. 2:5, 9; Heb. 7:11–12.

When too many believers are living in the first two columns in diagram 1, Hosea 4:6 applies:

My people are destroyed for lack of knowledge. Because you have rejected knowledge, I will also reject you from being My priest ...

When enough believers are living in the last column and therefore exerting the proper influence on the priest nation, God blesses the nation:

> *Malachi 3:7, 12 – ... return to Me and I will return to*
> *you ... And all the nations will call you blessed, for*
> *you shall be a delightful land, says the Lord of hosts*
> *[Lord of armies].*

Personal Implications: We are to advance to spiritual maturity or face loss of blessings/rewards:

> *1 Cor. 6:9 – ... do you not know that the unrighteous*
> *[believer] shall not inherit the kingdom*
> *Eph. 5:15 – ... be careful how you walk [walk in the*
> *Power Zone] ...*
> *Heb. 5:12 – ... by now, you should be teachers, but*
> *you need someone to teach you again the fundamental*
> *principles of the word of God ...*
> *Heb. 6:1 – ... leaving the elementary teaching about*
> *Christ, let us advance to maturity*

Eternal Implications: There will be no equality in heaven among believers:

> *Luke 8:18 – ... for whoever has [Divine good], to him*
> *shall be given; and whoever has not, from him shall*
> *be taken [human good] even that which he thinks he*
> *has.*
> *Isaiah 53:12 – ... He shall divide the spoil [eternal*
> *rewards] with the strong.*
> *Rom. 2:6 – ... render to each one according to his*
> *deeds.*

Blessings in time and rewards in eternity depend entirely on our choice of soul-control. The Christian life is about choices. With spiritual growth, the choices are often between good and good. But we face daily choices between good and bad ... between spiritual life and spiritual death ... between fellowship with God and separation from God. Because we face critical choices on a daily basis, there is no substitute for getting our priorities straight.

> *Prov. 1:7 – The fear of the Lord is the beginning of knowledge. Fools despise wisdom and instruction.*

> *Prov. 2:2–7 – Make your ear attentive to wisdom. Incline your heart to understanding; for if you cry for discernment, lift your voice for understanding; if you seek her as silver, and search for her as for hidden treasures; then you will discern the fear of the Lord, and discover the knowledge of God. For the Lord gives wisdom; from His mouth come knowledge and understanding. He stores up sound wisdom for the upright; He is a shield to those who walk in integrity.*

> *Prov. 3:5–6 – Trust in the Lord with all your heart, and do not lean on your own understanding. In all your ways acknowledge Him, and He will make your paths straight.*

> *Prov. 3:13–15 – How blessed is the man who finds wisdom, and the man who gains understanding. For its profit is better than the profits of silver, and its gain than fine gold. She is more precious than jewels, and nothing you desire compares with her.*

Soul-Control: Two Choices

We have a choice of being controlled by God through His Spirit inside the Power Zone or being controlled by our sin nature in one of the spiritual death zones. Diagram 2 explains.

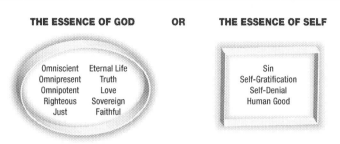

Only a foolish believer would choose soul-control by the essence of self, but that's what we all do when we decide to live in any of the spiritual death zones. As you can see by looking at the essence of God, He cannot possibly want anything but the very best for us. The problem is, we frequently think we have a better plan, and we take action to facilitate our own agenda. When we pursue our own agenda instead of God's, the stress on our soul eventually becomes unbearable. God did not design our souls to be pounded into oblivion by self-induced-misery, Divine discipline, scar tissue, and a hardened heart.

Take a really good look at the essence of God in diagram 2. If you had to come up with just one word that summarizes all ten characteristics, what would it be? To my mind, the word is "perfection." How can a perfect God have anything but a perfect plan for our lives? We will never know what His perfect plan for our lives is until we begin to grow spiritually and learn to live, work, and play inside the Power Zone. God is not going to lay out a road map and show us our lives from the beginning of our journey until the end. He takes us one step at a time, and more often than not, we're not certain what our next step will be. He expects us to look at His ten characteristics, none of which we possess, and make daily decisions to follow His lead. And how does God lead? He leads through knowledge and application of His word as taught and prompted by the Spirit. We can't apply to our daily lives what we don't know, we can't learn apart from being taught, and the Spirit doesn't teach us or prompt us unless we are inside the Power Zone. Keep in mind that when the Spirit directs our life, He has exactly the same ten characteristics as the Father and the Son. All three members of the Trinity have exactly the same essence, differing only in function.

The Principle of "Much More than the Most"

If God did the most for us at salvation when we were His enemies (unbelievers), then how can He do less for us now that we are His friends (believers)?

> *Rom. 5:10 – For if while we were enemies, we were reconciled to God through the death of His Son, much more, having been reconciled, we shall be saved by His life.*

Not only are we saved by faith in Christ, Christ came that we might have a more abundant life:

> *Jn. 10:10b – ... I came that they might have life, and might have it abundantly.*

> *Rom. 8:32 – He who did not spare His own Son, but delivered Him up for us all, how will He not also with Him freely give us all things.*

James tells us that there is a more abundant grace available to those believers who have submitted their will to Him and are advancing spiritually:

> *James 4: 6–8 – But He gives a greater grace. Therefore it says, "God is opposed to the proud, but gives grace to the humble." Submit therefore to God. Resist the devil and he will flee from you. Draw near to God and He will draw near to you.*

It should be obvious that God can only do "much more than the most" for us now that we are His friends. Let us never doubt that God desires to bless us. He is patiently waiting on high, eager to bring blessings into our lives:

> *Isaiah 30:18 – Therefore the Lord longs to be gracious to you, and therefore He waits on high to have compassion on you. For the Lord is a God of justice; how blessed are those who long for Him.*

God cannot bless us when we are controlled by our sin nature. If we want His blessing and compassion, we need to get back in fellowship with Him through confession of sin:

> *Proverbs 28:13; 1:23 – He who conceals his sins will not prosper, but he who confesses and forsakes them will find compassion. Turn to My reproof [confession of sin], and I will pour out My Spirit on you.*

If God is so anxious to bless us and extend to us greater grace when we are back in fellowship with Him, who or what is He waiting for? Or is it that He is looking for something? The answer is that He is doing both. He is still waiting on us, and He's looking at our hearts. He is waiting until He sees in our hearts what He wants to see.

> *Jer. 17:10; Ps. 44:21– I the Lord search the heart ... He knows the secrets of the heart.*

> *Heb. 4:12 – For the word of God is alive and powerful ... and able to judge the thoughts and intentions of the heart.*

When the righteousness of God sees what He wants to see in our hearts, the justice of God is mandated to bring abundant blessings into our life. He will start pouring into our cup until it overflows with blessings.

Psalms 23:5–6 – You prepare a table before me in the presence of my enemies; You anoint my head with oil; my cup runs over. Surely goodness and mercy shall follow me all the days of my life; and I will dwell in the house of the Lord forever.

Building a Spiritual House inside Our Soul

Both in adversity and in prosperity, David knew the source of his comfort and his blessings. That's why he is called "a man after God's own heart," 1 Sam. 13:14, and "the apple of God's eye," Ps. 17:8. In other words, David had a "spiritual house" inside his soul that the righteousness and justice of God was compelled to bless. However, as Church Age spiritual royalty, we have a much better opportunity to build a spiritual house inside our soul than David ever did. David did not have the permanent indwelling of the Spirit, nor the permanently available Power Zone in which to live, work, and play. Let's examine some verses concerning the building of our spiritual house.

Prov. 24:3–4 – By wisdom a house is stabilized, and by understanding it is established; and by knowledge the rooms are filled with all precious and pleasant riches.

Eph. 2:20; 1 Pet. 2:5 – ... having been built upon the foundation ... Christ Jesus Himself being the chief corner stone ... you also as living stones, are being built up as a spiritual house for a holy priesthood ...

Eph. 4:23; 3:17 – ... that you be renewed in the spirit of your mind [faith transfer to the human spirit] ... so that Christ may make a home in your hearts through faith [faith cycle to the right lobe].

It should be obvious that as Christ followers, we are to be in the construction business. We are to be constructing a spiritual house inside our own soul through the teaching ministry of the Spirit. Studying diagram 3 should illustrate how this actually happens, but before doing so, it would help considerably to go back to chapter 3, diagram 6, and review the three synergetic purposes of the human spirit.

DIAGRAM 3: GOD'S GRACE PERCEPTION AND APPLICATTION SYSTEM

God's Word + Spirit's Power
1 Jn. 1:9; 1 Cor. 2:14-15

Jer. 17:10; Mat. 5:8; Eph. 3:17;
1 Cor. 2:13; 2 Cor. 3:2-3; 1 Tim. 1:5

IQ Left Lobe

SPIRITUAL HOUSE
1 Pet. 1:5; Prov. 24:3-4;
Eph. 2:20-22

HEART Right Lobe

Faith Transfer
Heb. 4:2

HUMAN SPIRIT
Eph. 1:17

Faith Cycle
Eph. 3:17
Jn. 14:26

Holy Spirit Teaches Human Spirit
Rom. 8:16; 1 Cor. 2:10-14

Human Spirit: Foundation, Target, and Storehouse
Col. 2:7; Eph. 3:17, 20-21

When we take in God's word under the Spirit's power, the Spirit teaches the word to the human spirit. As long as we remain under the Spirit's power, God's word is cycled into the right lobe (heart) for application to our circumstances. Notice five very important things about this process:

1. God bypasses human I.Q. and teaches our human spirit in order to level the field.
2. There is not one ounce of human merit involved anywhere in this grace perception and application process.
3. Application of God's word to our circumstances occurs from the right lobe, which the Bible calls "the heart." God is always looking at our hearts because that is where our values are. *Mat. 6:21 – For where your treasure is, there your heart will be also.*

4. God does not bless us because of our human I.Q., but because of our spiritual I.Q., which is the content of our human spirit cycled through faith into our heart.
    Prov. 23:7 – As a man thinks in his heart [right lobe], *so he is.*
5. If we are not taking in the word of God consistently, there is nothing for the Holy Spirit to transfer into our human spirit and then cycle into our right lobe for application.

The Faith-Rest Process

There are several reasons the grace perception and application system breaks down. The basic reason is failure to confess sins and get back in the Power Zone, where the teaching ministry of the Spirit is operational. But another critical reason is failure to believe God's word. Lack of faith stops the transfer process. Hebrews chapter 4 addresses this problem of lack of faith:

> *Heb. 4:2b; 4:1 – ... but the word they heard did not profit them because it was not united by faith in those who heard. Therefore, since a promise remains [unclaimed] of entering His rest, let us fear ...*

In this passage, we are actually told to fear the failure to believe and therefore to claim the promises of God. God has given us over seven thousand promises in the Bible. Promises are to be used daily, but we cannot claim promises that we don't know. Failure to claim promises means living our lives in fear, worry, and anxiety, all of which are devastating mental-attitude sins. Mental-attitude sins cause self-induced misery, just for starters, and as we have seen in the previous chapter, it goes downhill from there.

As diagram 3 shows, if there is no "faith transfer" to the human spirit, there is also no "faith cycle" to the right lobe. And if there is no faith cycle to the right lobe (heart), then there is no faith rest. What's faith rest? Faith rest is claiming the promises of God so you can remain inside the Power Zone, by "resting" on the promises. Diagram 4 will help explain the faith rest process.

DIAGRAM 4: Faith Transfer – Faith Cycle – Faith Rest

Any successful athlete will tell you that rest is absolutely essential to athletic success. Many an athletic battle has been lost because fatigue overcame talent.

Likewise, many a spiritual battle has been lost due to spiritual fatigue from failure to rest in the promises of God. Nothing wears us out like pressure without promises. If you cannot find a good book that breaks down the promises of God into categories, then begin to develop your own "promise notebook" so you have some firepower against the missiles of the enemy.

Be advised that faith rest is just one of the categories for application of God's word, but it's one of the more important categories for at least two fundamental reasons: (1) Faith rest helps us to remain in the Power Zone; (2) Faith rest is the backbone of our prayer life. Effective prayer means believing that God can and will answer our prayers.

> *Mat. 21:22 – And everything you ask in prayer, believing, you shall receive.*

Also of great importance: faith rest doesn't mean that we do nothing. It means we do everything possible to bring about what we think is God's will for our lives, and once having done so, rest on the promises of God, knowing that God is working on our behalf as He simultaneously builds us into the person He wants us to be.

> *2 Pet. 1:3–4 – ... seeing that His divine power has granted to us everything pertaining to life and godliness, through the true knowledge of Him who called us by His own glory and excellence. For by these He has granted to us His precious and magnificent promises, in order that by them you might become partakers of the divine nature ...*

God makes it very clear that we are not to live our lives like a ship on stormy seas without an anchor or a navigation system:

> *Eph. 4:14 – ... we are no longer to be children, tossed about by waves, and carried about by every wind of false doctrine, by the cunning craftiness of deceitful schemers.*

Instead of drowning in despair in the storms of life, we can anchor our lives with promises, dance in the storms, and enjoy the cruise.

A VISUAL MODEL FOR OUR SPIRITUAL HOUSE

As we step up our faith rest drill and begin to apply the promises of God, we are continuing the process of constructing within our soul the spiritual house of diagrams 3 and 4. Our spiritual house is to be filled with all categories of spiritual knowledge, Eph. 3:16–18.

What does our spiritual house look like? How many floors does it have? What type of furniture is inside it? To this day, the best and probably the only spiritual house model I have ever seen was developed by Col. Thieme (see the acknowledgments) many years ago. He called it "The Edification Complex of the Soul." The word "edification" (*oikodome*) means "to build a home," and in the spiritual sense refers to spiritual growth, Eph. 2:22; 3:16, 19, 4:23; Col. 2:7; 1 Tim. 1:5; 1 Pet. 2:5; Prov. 24:3–4. One of the great things about the spiritual house model is that it gives us an idea where we may be with regard to our personal spiritual maturity. While only God knows for sure exactly where we are spiritually, the colonel's model will at least give us some benchmarks.

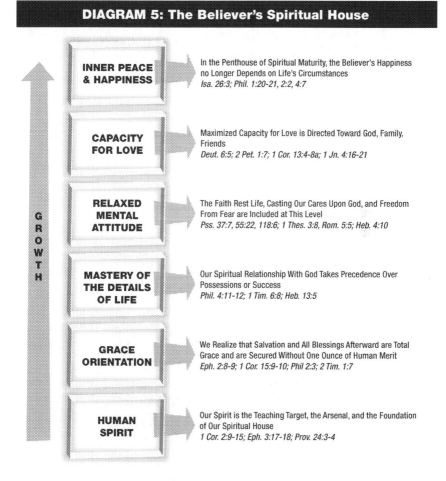

DIAGRAM 5: The Believer's Spiritual House

INNER PEACE & HAPPINESS
In the Penthouse of Spiritual Maturity, the Believer's Happiness no Longer Depends on Life's Circumstances
Isa. 26:3; Phil. 1:20-21, 2:2, 4:7

CAPACITY FOR LOVE
Maximized Capacity for Love is Directed Toward God, Family, Friends
Deut. 6:5; 2 Pet. 1:7; 1 Cor. 13:4-8a; 1 Jn. 4:16-21

RELAXED MENTAL ATTITUDE
The Faith Rest Life, Casting Our Cares Upon God, and Freedom From Fear are Included at This Level
Pss. 37:7, 55:22, 118:6; 1 Thes. 3:8, Rom. 5:5; Heb. 4:10

MASTERY OF THE DETAILS OF LIFE
Our Spiritual Relationship With God Takes Precedence Over Possessions or Success
Phil. 4:11-12; 1 Tim. 6:8; Heb. 13:5

GRACE ORIENTATION
We Realize that Salvation and All Blessings Afterward are Total Grace and are Secured Without One Ounce of Human Merit
Eph. 2:8-9; 1 Cor. 15:9-10; Phil 2:3; 2 Tim. 1:7

HUMAN SPIRIT
Our Spirit is the Teaching Target, the Arsenal, and the Foundation of Our Spiritual House
1 Cor. 2:9-15; Eph. 3:17-18; Prov. 24:3-4

GROWTH

As we advance spiritually toward the penthouse, our maturity levels will be tested. However, God has promised us He will never test us beyond our capabilities:

1 Cor. 10:13 – No temptation has overtaken you but such as is common to man; and God is faithful, who will not allow you to be tempted beyond what you are able, but with the temptation will provide the way of escape also, that you may be able to endure it.

God will not test us at the penthouse level when our spiritual maturity level is only on one of the lower floors, such as grace orientation. God is fair, and He knows exactly what we can handle. Although God will not test us beyond our capabilities, obviously we can place ourselves in harm's way. If we find ourselves failing tests on a regular basis, then we are neglecting to apply God's word, making bad decisions about where we should be, hanging with the wrong crowd, etc. If that's the case, then we need to make some lifestyle changes. By not doing so, we are placing ourselves at the mercy of the world, the flesh, and the devil. The only place we can gain victory over these three enemies of freedom is inside the Power Zone.

Regardless of where you are spiritually right now, or where you have been, God is more concerned with where you want to go. Even if you have been in the Stone Zone and under the threat of the sin unto death, the option of exploiting grace in the Phone Zone through confession of sin is still available to you. You can get out of the Stone Zone and back into the Power Zone through the grace provision of the Phone Zone. If you truly desire to renew your relationship with God, you need to have every confidence that what He is going to do for Israel in the future He can do for you right now:

> *Ezek. 11:19–20 – ... I will take the stony heart out of their flesh ... That they may walk in My statutes and keep My ordinances ... they will be My people, and I shall be their God.*

If you are concerned that so much of your life has been lived in the spiritual death zones that it's just too late for you, then God has more promises for you:

> *Phil. 3:13 – ... forgetting what lies behind and reaching forward to what lies ahead*

> *Joel 2:12–13, 25 – ... Return to Me with all your heart ... return to the Lord your God, for He is gracious and compassionate, slow to anger, abounding in loving kindness ... I will make up to you for the years that the swarming locust has eaten ...*

We don't fully comprehend how God can make up to us the years we have wasted or even the years we were sort of "in neutral" and not really advancing spiritually. But when God promises something, we can take it to the bank. God has never broken a promise! When we look at His essence in diagram 2, it is obvious that it is impossible for Him to fail to keep His word. Consider that only God can take all the events of our life, both the good and the bad, and cause everything to work together for good. Let's look again at our old friend, Romans 8:28:

> *And we know that God causes all things to work together for good to those who love God, to those who are called according to His purpose.*

You will notice that there actually is a contingency that goes with this verse. The contingency phrase is "to those who love God." So the contingency to Rom. 8:28 is that we must grow spiritually, according to His predetermined plan, to the point where we actually love God.

What Does It Mean To Love God?

To be sure, there are varying degrees of capacity for loving God, based upon our level of spiritual maturity. The secret to love can be summed up in one word: capacity. The greater our spiritual maturity, the greater our capacity to love God. But God doesn't give us a capacity requirement in Romans 8:28; He just says, "to those who love God." That tells me that even for baby believers who remain positive toward the word, God is going to work things together for good in their lives. All believers who remain positive will eventually grow into spiritual adolescence and then spiritual maturity. So what is the real issue behind Romans 8:28? The real issue in loving God is consistency of spiritual growth, which takes us back to the Parable of the Sower, doesn't it?

In diagram 1, the Parable of the Sower, the believers in the first two columns are part of the "spin-off"—they have taken themselves out of the spiritual maturity race, and they are on their own except for the grace God extends to keep them physically alive. Romans 8:28 does not apply to them until and unless they return to the Power Zone through the Phone Zone, confession of sin. Even then, they have to remain consistent in their spiritual growth, or they will return to living in the spiritual death zones. Therefore, Romans 8:28 applies only to those living in the last column, those who have committed their lives to following Christ.

Imagine having the opportunity to live under the promise of Romans 8:28 and failing to exploit grace in the Power Zone! Imagine failing to claim the promise of Joel 2:25, that God can restore the years the locust has eaten! Imagine declining the invitation of God in Ezek. 11:19 to take us out of the Stone Zone and heal our hardened heart! Regardless of where you are spiritually—a baby believer to the habitual hard case in the Stone Zone—God still has a plan for your life, or you would be dead.

What Can We Expect from God?

God has issued us a standing invitation: open the door to the Phone Zone, come back into the Power Zone, grow spiritually, and let the Spirit direct our lives! Once we have decided to do that and we are back in a spiritual growth pattern under the ministry of gifted Bible teachers, what can we expect from God? Gradually, over a period of consistent growth under the teaching ministry of the Spirit, God will begin to heal what needs to be healed, develop what needs to be developed, empower what needs to be empowered, and bless what needs to be blessed.

*Phil. 4:19 – Now my God shall fill up the deficiency
of all your need according to the standard of His
riches in glory in Christ Jesus.*

In verse 19, the phrase "fill up the deficiency" is the Greek word
pleroo' (play-ro-oh), a word that is absolutely loaded with spiritual
significance. It means four things:

1. To fill up a deficiency – We come to God with nothing but
    a sin nature. Once we accept Christ as Savior, He begins to
    fill up our deficiency of soul, as Divine viewpoint begins to
    replace human viewpoint.

    *Phil. 2:5; Rom. 12:2 – Let this mind be in you which was
    also in Christ Jesus. And do not be conformed to this world,
    but be transformed by the renewing of your mind, that you
    may prove what the will of God is, that which is good and
    acceptable and perfect.*

2. To fill with a certain quality – There's something about the
    believer oriented to grace and in possession of a relaxed
    mental attitude that attracts those missing these qualities.

    *Phil. 4:7 – And the peace of God, which surpasses all
    understanding, shall guard your hearts and minds in Christ
    Jesus.*

3. To fully influence – As we begin to grow spiritually, we are
    actually constructing a spiritual fortress inside our soul. The
    result is stability in our lives.

    *Prov. 24:3–4 – By wisdom a house is built, and by
    understanding it is stabilized. And by knowledge the rooms
    are filled with all precious and pleasant riches.*

4. To fully possess – The foundation of the spiritual house
    being constructed inside our soul is called the human

spirit. We become fully possessed by God's word when our human spirit is saturated with Bible doctrine and we cycle doctrine into our heart (right lobe) for application to our circumstances.

Eph. 3:16–19 – that He would grant you, according to the riches of His glory, to be strengthened with power through His Spirit in the inner man; so that Christ may dwell in your hearts through faith; and that you, being rooted and grounded in love, may be able to comprehend with all believers what is the breadth and length and height and depth, and to know the love of Christ which surpasses knowledge, that you may be filled up to all the fullness [pleroo] of God.

The terms *breadth, length, height, and depth* all describe the different compartments of the human spirit that the teaching ministry of the Holy Spirit fills up with different categories of God's word. When we are in the Power Zone and taking in the word of God, the Holy Spirit is busy "sorting out" the categories of doctrine and placing them into the right compartments of our human spirit, Eph. 3:18. The Spirit works tirelessly for us so that we can apply the appropriate categories of doctrine to different circumstances and thereby have meaning, purpose, and definition to our lives.

Imagine, for a moment, being God and knowing from eternity past all of our personal sins, failures, mistakes, weaknesses, tragic decisions, as well as all the repercussions in our own life and in the lives of others. Though He knew all these things before we ever existed, imagine the grace and the love he must experience to have granted us the privilege of human life. Imagine the omniscience that took all our shortcomings into consideration and still designed a perfect plan for our life. Imagine a grace so comprehensive that it is greater than the sum total of all our failures.

Having considered God's grace, do we want to live in the spiritual death zones or exploit the grace of God in the Power Zone? While Satan is throwing all his best pitches trying to strike us out, living inside the Power Zone gives us the opportunity to break the record for spiritual home runs. So what are we waiting for? Step up to the plate!

CHAPTER 8 KEY POINTS

- Dispensations are divisions of human history designed by God in eternity past to facilitate the progressive revelation of His comprehensive plan. (p. 163)
- The Power Zone was never available to believers until the Church Age because Christ had not yet demonstrated its power. (p. 164)
- Only Church Age believers are in union with Christ. We are spiritual royalty. (p. 165)
- The Parable of the Sower has national, personal, and eternal implications. (p. 167-168)
- We have two choices concerning who controls our soul: the essence of God, or the essence of self. (p. 170, diagram 2)
- Christ followers are to be in the construction business, constructing a spiritual house inside of our souls. (p. 174, diagram 3)
- Faith rest is claiming the promises of God so we can remain inside the Power Zone by "resting" on His promises. (p. 176, diagram 4)
- Over a period of consistent growth under the teaching ministry of the Spirit, God will begin to heal what needs to be healed, develop what needs to be developed, empower what needs to be empowered, and bless what needs to be blessed. (p. 182)

GLOSSARY

Baptism of the Spirit – A one-time status-bringing event that occurs at the moment of salvation when God the Holy Spirit places the new believer into permanent union with Jesus Christ inside the Security Zone.

Bone Zone – The fourth and final spiritual death zone in which the unrepentant believer is removed by God through the sin unto death.

Carnality – The absolute state of soul in which the sin nature is 100 percent in control.

Christianity – A relationship with all three members of the Trinity, secured through faith in Christ, maintained by choice, and totally dependent upon the character and grace of God.

Church Age – The current dispensation that began on the Day of Pentecost and will terminate with the Rapture of the church.

Clone Zone – The first spiritual death zone in which the believer has just chosen to sin, therefore grieving the Spirit and transferring soul-control from the Holy Spirit back to the sin nature. This is the zone in which self-induced misery and warning discipline begins.

Cosmos diabolicus – The devil's world and all its systems.

Dispensations – Divisions of human history designed by God in eternity past to facilitate the progressive revelation of His comprehensive grace plan to benefit man.

Divine discipline – God's punishment of the carnal believer, designed to motivate the believer to return to fellowship with Him inside the Power Zone.

Doctrine – The word of God.

Double-minded – The believer whose lifestyle is like a yo-yo— swinging back and forth between the Power Zone and the spiritual death zones.

Dying discipline – The believer under maximum Divine discipline in the Stone Zone and therefore flirting with the sin unto death.

Empowerment of the Spirit – The unprecedented empowerment of the Church Age believer by the Holy Spirit for the purpose of living the Spirit-Directed Life. Although universally and permanently available for all Church Age believers, empowerment is lost through sin and regained only through confession of sin.

Enduement – Limited empowerment by the Spirit provided for a few Old Testament believers to perform specific tasks for certain periods of time. Enduement was neither universally nor permanently available.

Faith rest – A major technique for Christian living in which the believer claims the promises of God and "rests" on the promises, thereby enjoying tranquility of soul.

Fellowship with God – Rapport with God beginning at the moment of salvation, interrupted by sin, and resumed through confession of sin.

Filling of the Spirit – Synonymous with "Empowerment of the Spirit."

Grace – Everything that God is free to do for man based on the work of Christ on the cross.

Groan Zone – The second spiritual death zone in which the believer has quenched the Spirit by refusing to confess sin. The zone in which the frantic search for happiness, scar tissue of the soul, and intensified Divine discipline begins.

Human good – Any good deeds performed by an unbeliever or by a believer who is out of fellowship with God. All human good is powered by the sin nature.

Human spirit – The spirit created by the Holy Spirit inside the believer's soul at the moment of salvation. Has a threefold purpose: Target for the teaching ministry of the Holy Spirit; Storehouse for categorical doctrines; Arsenal for spiritual warfare. Also serves as the foundation of the "spiritual house" being constructed inside the growing believer's soul.

Immoral degeneracy – A lifestyle of catering to the sin and self-gratification areas of the sin nature.

Indwelling of the Spirit – The permanent residence of God the Holy Spirit inside the body and soul of the Church Age believer. Accompanies the believer's permanent residence in the Security Zone.

Intensified discipline – The second stage of progressive Divine discipline administered by God to the believer living in the Groan Zone due to the believer's refusal or failure to confess sin.

Mental-attitude sins – The starting point of verbal and overt sins. Is exemplified by pride, jealousy, hatred, anger, fear, worry, guilt, judging, bitterness, self-pity, and various lusts.

Moral degeneracy – A lifestyle of counterfeiting spirituality through the sin nature's areas of human good and self-denial.

Pentecost – The day on which the Church Age began, ten days after the ascension of Christ, and marked by the giving of the Holy Spirit.

Phone Zone – The zone in which the repentant believer "phones home" through confession of sin in order to recover fellowship with God and the empowerment ministries of the Spirit.

Power Zone –The grace-provided, exclusive spiritual dimension in which fellowship with God, Spirit empowerment, spiritual growth, production, and effective prayer become operational.

Priest nation – A representative status extended by God to any Gentile nation in the Church Age that will:

- Protect the freedom of the church to spread the gospel of Christ and to teach God's Word
- Protect its citizen's rights to human life, freedom, privacy, and property
- Provide a haven of toleration and protection for Jews at home and abroad
- Serve as a base for missionary activity to foreign countries open to the gospel of Christ

Progressive Divine discipline – The discipline administered by God to the unrepentant believer who continues in spiritual degeneration across the zones of spiritual death. The progression consists of warning discipline, intensified discipline, and dying discipline, culminating if necessary with the sin unto death.

Remnant – Believers who make up the backbone of any priest nation because they have a lifestyle of persistent spiritual growth and production.

Salvation – The grace gift of eternal life offered by God through faith alone in Christ alone.

Scar tissue – Darkening of the soul caused by disobedience or rejection of God's word, as in Eph. 4:18. Scar tissue first begins to form in the Groan Zone and accelerates in the Stone Zone.

Security Zone – The exalted position of permanent relationship with the Trinity awarded to every believer in Christ at the moment of salvation.

Self-denial – A production of the sin nature in which you deny yourself legitimate things in the false assumption that it will enhance spirituality and bring you closer to God.

Self-gratification – Catering to any of the lust trends of your sin nature.

Sin – Any thought, statement, or deed emanating from the soul of man that violates the character or commandments of God.

Sin nature – The ever-present enticement, living inside the cellular structure of human beings, seeking to violate the character or commandments of God.

Sin unto death – The epitome of Divine discipline in which God removes a believer from this world. Occurs when the believer has accumulated maximum scar tissue and hardness of the heart from living in the Stone Zone.

Soul-control – The ever-present choice of the believer to be controlled by the Holy Spirit or by the sin nature.

Spiritual death – The perpetual state of any unbeliever as separated from God, or the temporary separation from God of any believer who has committed an act of personal sin.

Spiritual life – The spiritual status of any believer at the moment of salvation, and the status of the repentant believer who has squared his or her account with God through confession of sin.

Spiritual gifts – The gifts given to the believer by the Holy Spirit at the moment of salvation, empowered only by the Spirit, and enhanced through spiritual growth.

Spiritual house – The multilevel structure inside the soul that is erected on the foundation of the human spirit through the teaching ministry of the Holy Spirit.

Spiritual I.Q. – The amount of Bible doctrine residing in the compartments of the human spirit and right lobe (heart), and therefore instantly available for application to our circumstances.

Spirituality – The absolute state of soul of the believer in which the Holy Spirit is 100 percent in control.

Stone Zone – The third and final spiritual death zone characterized by maximized self-induced misery, scar tissue of the soul, hardness of the heart, and dying discipline.

Tongues – The temporary spiritual gift of evangelizing dispersed and unbelieving Jews in Gentile languages as a disciplinary warning that their priest nation status would soon be revoked.

The Trinity – The Godhead of identical and perfect character consisting of the Father as the author of the grace plan for humankind, the Son as the Savior and executor of the plan, and the Holy Spirit as the empowerment and revealer of the plan.

Warning discipline – The "Clone Zone" stage of Divine discipline in which God warns the believer to get back in fellowship with Him immediately through the grace provision of confession of sin (the Phone Zone).